SCIENCE FOR EXCELLENCE

LEVEL 4

physical science

Scottish Schools Science Group

Series Editors:
Nicky Souter, Paul Chambers and Stephen Jeffrey

Authors:
Paul Chambers and Tom Clark

DYNAMIC LEARNING

HODDER GIBSON

Contents

Introduction

Science for Excellence Level 4: Physical Science is directed towards the Level Four Science experiences and outcomes of Curriculum for Excellence in Scotland. Its main focus is on those relating to the Forces, Electricity and Waves organiser, but it also encompasses a number of the outcomes in the Planet Earth organiser. It was felt that much could be addressed in this section from a physical science perspective that is different from the traditional recall of factual content regarding the Solar System. It makes frequent reference to key concepts identified in Curriculum for Excellence and the topics chosen in the text can be linked with content across the other organisers.

Although the chapters are designed to meet Curriculum for Excellence Level Four outcomes, their approach and content have also been influenced by the need to articulate with National Four and National Five developments which were underway at the time of writing. An enquiry-based approach suggests activities which are designed to encourage pupils to plan and design experiments which present opportunities for individual investigation or practical challenges but also others which are more designed to provide progression onto the next stage. This is reflected in the inclusion of content covering forces, gas laws, sound and electricity.

In an attempt to allow our pupils to make more informed decisions on scientific issues relating to their own experiences, the chapters have a strong Scottish viewpoint, but this is balanced by reference to global issues. It is hoped that the physical science content, presented alongside examples of historical ideas, will develop pupils' awareness of science as a continuing process involving tentative ideas, and that what is considered correct at one time may be refined in light of new discoveries.

Some of the activities in the book involve experiments. These should only be attempted under the instruction of the Science Teacher and in accordance with the appropriate safety guidelines. Problems and activities are designed to examine and extend the content of the chapters. Skills in literacy and numeracy as well as an awareness of the importance of health and wellbeing will be developed through these exercises – look out for the icons shown at the end of this Introduction. Some chapters allow for numerical and graphical activities while others seek to reinforce the scientific principles contained in the main text. It was also felt that in an attempt to make the learners more active participants, open-ended and pupil investigation activities should feature. These activities encourage individual project work, research and group work, with learners being asked to make informed decisions on scientific advances which may have ethical or societal implications. The tasks are designed around the 'broad features of assessment in science'.

The principles and practices outlined in Curriculum for Excellence have been adopted throughout the *Science for Excellence* series. The series is designed to be used in conjunction with schemes of work which reflect learning and teaching approaches which are most applicable to the sciences.

The series provides opportunities for scientific enquiry and examples of scientific scenarios where pupils can, for example, link variables to determine relationships or improve their scientific thinking or make informed judgements on the basis of scientific principles.

Scientifically Literate Citizens

The series' use of real data and experimental type situations is designed to support the development of pupils' scientific attitudes. They will be able to look at data critically, make informed judgements on the basis of these and be critical and analytical of the science as well as the implications of broad or bold claims. Our scientific and technological development in various areas and at various times is recorded, and the impact of those developments is seen in context and as an indication of how our society has used and managed science for our benefit.

A significant challenge for Curriculum for Excellence and the *Science for Excellence* series is to change our pupils' attitudes to science and to help them become more able to engage positively in issues that will affect them. It is intended that the series' approach and content will help them to appreciate the scientific challenges and issues facing mankind and to respond in critical and informed ways. Enquiry, scepticism, analysis and questioning lie at the heart of 'real' science; we offer, in the text and within the selected images, some of the dilemmas facing science and society. These require continual revisiting and further scrutiny.

Science for Excellence strives to act as a sound preparatory text for pupils, including those progressing to the next stage, providing a secure understanding of the key issues in science.

We are inspired by science and its impact on our lives. We have been motivated by the pupils and new teachers we have taught, our colleagues in schools. Teachers are, outside the family, the most important influence on young people; the quality of their work is frequently underestimated and *Science for Excellence* is offered to support their challenging work. We are grateful for the patience and constant support of the outstanding team at Hodder Gibson as well as those closest to us.

Nicky Souter, Paul Chambers and Stephen Jeffrey
Series Editors
Science for Excellence
2011

 Literacy

 Numeracy

 Health and wellbeing

PLANET EARTH
Energy sources and sustainability

Energy generation in Scotland

Level 3 — What came before?

 SCN 3-04b

By investigating renewable energy sources and taking part in practical activities to harness them, I can discuss their benefits and potential problems.

Level 4 — What is this chapter about?

 SCN 4-04a

By contributing to an investigation on different ways of meeting society's energy needs, I can express an informed view on the risks and benefits of different energy sources, including those produced from plants.

 SCN 4-04b

Through investigation, I can explain the formation and use of fossil fuels and contribute to discussions on the responsible use and conservation of finite resources.

Energy generation in Scotland

Scotland and its energy

Scotland currently is in a relatively good position to provide the energy it requires for the foreseeable future. Our energy is supplied by a combination of nuclear and fossil-fuelled power stations and a number of renewable sources.

Our high voltage electrical transmission network is connected to systems in England and Northern Ireland. Since 2005 our energy generation and transmission system has been integrated into the wider British electricity trading market. As a result we have been exporting electrical energy to our neighbours.

The amount of electrical energy we produce however is not just down to how much we *can* produce but is also linked to what the United Kingdom and the rest of the Europe agrees is appropriate for the European energy policy. The Scottish Government has stated that it has a target for Scotland to produce 50% of its energy by renewable sources by 2020. It is entirely possible for Scotland to do this as there is great potential for continued development of onshore and possibly offshore wind power.

The development of which energy sources we need or should use in Europe is driven mainly by European Union-wide legislation, with the European Commission (EC) launching a wide range of initiatives to meet key climate-energy challenges.

In January 2008, the European Commission published proposals to achieve its environmental objectives relating to energy production. The Energy and Climate Package included:

- Achieving a 20% reduction in greenhouse gas emissions against 1990 levels. This target will probably increase to 30%.
- Supplying 20% of final energy consumption from renewable energy sources by 2020 (from 8.5% in 2005).

In addition, the European Union endorsed a goal to achieve a 20% improvement in energy efficiency by 2020. The Scottish Government has to decide in which areas to invest to meet the energy needs and also keep within the European guidelines.

A significant difference between Scotland and the rest of the United Kingdom is that the Scottish Government has stated it will not build any more nuclear power stations. For the rest of the United Kingdom nuclear power is seen as a key factor in providing our future energy.

What does this mean for Scotland and what could we do?

Our current maximum power production is approximately 12.1 **gigawatts** (GW).

Now 12.1 GW = 12 100 000 000 watts
= 12 100 000 000 Joules per second!

A hair dryer is about 1500 watts.
An electric shower could be 7000 watts.
A light bulb could be as little as 30 watts.

This 12.1 GW is generated in a range of power stations all over the country and is used to power our homes, factories, shops, workplaces and streetlights. Every time someone uses a kettle or switches on a television, energy is taken from one of these power stations. Operators in power stations watch the demand (what we use) and match this with the supply (what we generate).

The quest for renewables

The breakdown of our current energy production is shown in the following chart produced by the Scottish Government in 2009.

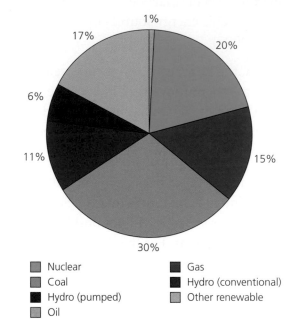

- Nuclear
- Coal
- Hydro (pumped)
- Oil
- Gas
- Hydro (conventional)
- Other renewable

It is difficult to accurately quantify the percentage produced by oil-fired power stations as Peterhead Power Station is a multi-fuel station and has recently been predominantly fuelled by gas.

Our renewable energy generation comes from a number of different sources and is currently approximately 3.5 GW. Its breakdown is shown in the following chart (2011).

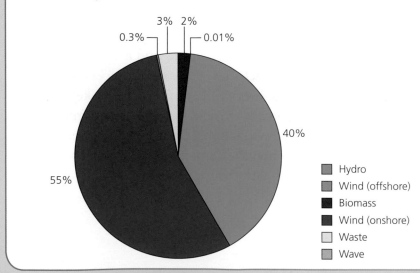

- Hydro
- Wind (offshore)
- Biomass
- Wind (onshore)
- Waste
- Wave

It can be seen that we obtain most of our renewable energy from wind and hydro sources. Newer technologies such as waste and biomass are in their infancy but are expected to increase greatly over the next few years.

The breakdown of energy generation from our renewable sources over the past few years is shown in the following bar chart.

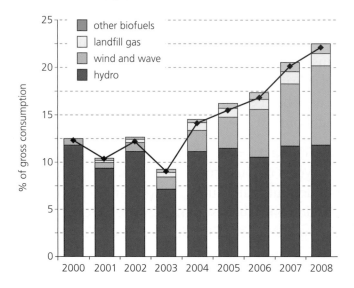

This chart shows the quite dramatic increase in our production of energy from wind and wave power and from **landfill** gas. Given the recent increase in wind farm construction in Scotland this figure is certain to rise.

Supply and demand

The issue of energy supply and demand is not simple. We are trying to reduce our energy consumption from fossil based fuels in an attempt to reduce our CO_2 emissions. These CO_2 emissions are felt by many to be linked to global warming so any reduction in fossil fuel use will reduce the emissions and also conserve a finite supply of fuel.

We could also try to be more efficient in our use of energy so as to reduce our costs and possibly be less reliant on imported oil or nuclear power.

The following chart shows our overall production of electrical energy in Scotland from all sources between 2000 and 2006.

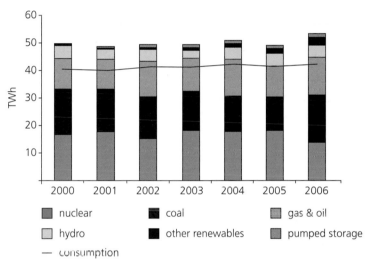

Note: other renewables includes wind, wave, solar power and thermal renewables

Patterns and trends can be seen but an interesting point is the line marked 'consumption'. This line is always below the total energy generated. This means we have always generated more energy than we require. It is this surplus that we can sell to other countries.

The future

The issue of increasing our renewable energy is of major importance to us. The Government tries to predict our supply and demand capabilities so we can ensure we have enough energy and also ensure our environment is not harmed or damaged. Many surveys and predictions are being undertaken in an attempt to forecast future requirements. One recent report on renewable energy has looked at previous figures, assessed our capabilities, and then made predictions on what is likely.

The future

These renewable energy generation forecasts are shown in the following table.

(MW)	2007/8	2008/9	2009/10	2010/11	2011/12	2012/13	2013/14	2014/15	2015+
Wind	1231	1721	3635	4808	4885	5666	6453	7124	10500
Hydro	1116	1158	1158	1158	1158	1158	1158	1165	1172
Biomass	45	97	97	97	97	97	97	97	97
Total	2392	2976	4890	6063	6140	6921	7708	8386	11769

As can be seen the general trend is for a gradual increase in overall production but with some sources growing more than others. Hydro does not increase dramatically if at all. Dams are very expensive to build and maintain.

As stated earlier, our renewable electricity generation capacity is about 3.5 GW. An additional capacity of more than 3.5 GW is either in construction or has received consent. The majority of this new capacity (96%) is expected from wind generation.

One forecast of our growth in renewables is shown in the following chart with projects currently installed, under construction, consented, in planning, or being considered seriously. This could take Scotland's potential renewable capacity to 14 GW. This is more than our current power need!

The development of all these renewable projects would result in Scotland passing its 2020 target (50% gross consumption from renewables) by a considerable margin.

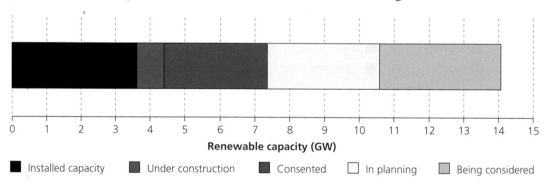

Renewable capacity (GW)

■ Installed capacity   ■ Under construction   ■ Consented   ☐ In planning   ■ Being considered

Active Learning ▶

Activities

1 📖 Design a presentation showing the main energy sources used in Scotland. This can be a poster or a slide on a computer. It should describe the types (renewable or not) and what fraction or how much energy is produced. Tables, charts or graphs should help you present your findings.

2 Much of our renewable energy is intended to be generated through wind power. This can be onshore or offshore. Which do you think is better and why?

3 Should Scotland have some nuclear power as well? Fewer people have been killed or injured compared with coal and gas power generation but nuclear is often mentioned with a big health warning. So why is nuclear power regarded as more dangerous by some?

4 ➗ Draw a bar chart showing the production of energy produced by wind from 2007/8 to 20012/13 in Scotland.

Electricity distribution

How does electric energy reach our homes and workplaces?

The map shows the main high voltage power lines and power stations throughout Scotland.

Scotland's terrain, weather, size and energy demands have led to the present combination of power generators currently in operation. The location of hydro-electric stations depends upon geography and rainfall patterns and this is reflected by the number of dams in mountainous areas. We currently have two nuclear power stations and a number of coal power stations. All of these generate electrical energy which is transferred to users via the **National Grid** which distributes the energy around the country.

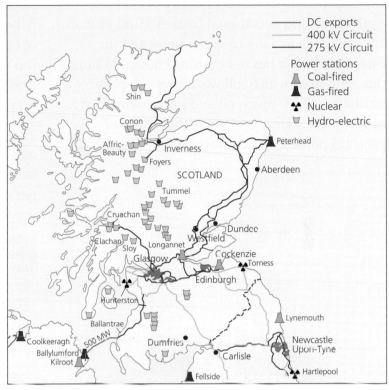

Map of power stations in Scotland (source: SCID Scotland's future energy 2008)

Oil and gas reserves

What reserves of fossil fuels remain for Scotland? (How long is a piece of string?)

The lifetime of the Scottish oil and gas industry will depend largely on **commodity** prices, exploration and operational costs. To find new oil and gas fields we have to spend more and the financial climate has to be strong enough to fund this. The chart which follows shows two possible estimates of how much oil and gas remain. This is not an exact science and is a combination of present knowledge and informed 'guesswork'.

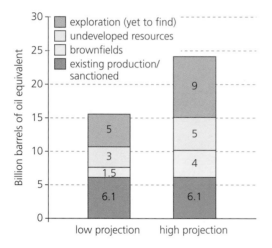

To give an indication of our own reserves of oil it is interesting to look at the oil extracted from the North Sea. We started to produce oil from about 1967 and by 2011 approximately 40 000 000 000 barrels of oil and gas will have been taken.

There is no exact answer to how much oil remains, but the government estimates that there may be between 15 000 000 000 and 24 000 000 000 barrels of oil and gas which could be recovered. This might change however if we were to invest more money in exploration.

Another major factor in how long the reserves may last is how much energy we use in our daily lives. If we were to reduce our energy consumption or increase our use of renewables, the remaining oil and gas reserves could last for much longer.

Other countries can also have an impact on the length of time the energy reserves will last. Many African countries for example are not heavy users of energy but if they were to become more industrialised they would require more. This would affect international prices and ultimately how much we could afford to buy.

The following table shows the relative amounts of oil each country uses. The final column shows how much fuel (in barrels) each country uses **per person per year**. (The abbreviation th.bar means thousands of barrels.)

Consuming nation 2008	th.bar/day	Population in millions	bar/year per person
United States	19 497.95	314	22.6
China	7 831.00	1345	2.1
Japan	4 784.85	127	13.7
India	2 962.00	1198	0.9
Russia	2 916.00	140	7.6
Germany	2 569.28	82	11.4
Brazil	2 485.00	193	4.7
Saudi Arabia (OPEC)	2 376.00	25	33.7
Canada	2 261.36	33	24.6
South Korea	2 174.91	48	16.4
Mexico	2 128.46	109	7.1
France	1 986.26	62	11.6
Iran (OPEC)	1 741.00	74	8.6
United Kingdom	1 709.66	61	10.1
Italy	1 639.01	60	10.0

Most non-industrialised countries have a figure of about 2 barrels per year per person. This means that on average each person in a country such as Zambia uses one fifth the amount of someone in Scotland or one tenth the amount of someone living in the United States. North American countries often use more energy during the summer months than during the winter months! Air conditioning units use large amounts of energy and large buildings, shopping centres, schools and factories can be difficult to keep cool. Millions of homes have these units too and they extract heat from inside buildings and release it to the outside which then increases the temperature of the air surrounding the buildings.

New technologies and biomass

Biomass is a renewable source of energy. The term biomass generally refers to biological material which was recently grown and then used to generate heat. A simple example of biomass is to cut down wood and use it in a fire. Much of our normal household waste can give off gas which can then be used for burning. Our landfill sites (where we dump household waste) give off this landfill gas which is flammable. As the waste decays it releases certain chemicals (liquid and gas) and it is these which can be used to generate heat.

Our biggest source of energy from wood comes from the liquid collected when wood is being pulped to produce paper. This liquid is capable of being burned and generating heat and so electrical energy. Many pulping factories use this liquid to power and heat the factory, in effect using the waste and 'recycling' it to reduce the waste being sent to other sites.

New technologies and biomass

Edible crops such as corn, maize and sugar cane can be altered chemically by **fermentation** to produce a type of alcohol which can then be used in cars and other vehicles. Left over or used vegetable oils and animal fats can be converted to biodiesel for use in trucks and other vehicles.

A great advantage of these fuels is the fact they are renewable. Corn and crops like these can be grown again year after year. (The same is true of trees but the time required is obviously much longer.) The land on which the crops are grown requires to be continually re-nourished, and this is a cost which has to be taken into account.

The technology needed to develop these fuels efficiently is not far advanced at the present but there is hope that it will improve greatly within the foreseeable future and so impact on our overall energy plan.

This van runs on 100% Biodiesel

FILTERTECHNIK
Biodiesel Purification Specialists
0800 068 4134
www.filtertechnik.co.uk/biodiesel

The use of peat

Recent fluctuations in the price of fossil fuels (oil and gas) have caused much concern in Britain and Europe but it wasn't always like this.

Scotland has had great supplies of a fuel called peat but as it was never developed fully we may not appreciate it. Our boggy, wet hillsides are ideal locations for the formation of this dark fibrous material which we call peat.

Peat is formed from partially decomposed plant matter, and can include trees, shrubs, herbs, sedges, grasses and mosses. Peat forms where plant remains are added at a greater rate than they are

The use of peat

broken down. That is, plants and grasses die and fall to the ground and begin to decompose. The following year more plant materials and water cover these decomposing grasses but stop fresh air from reaching them. In cool, waterlogged conditions, the lack of oxygen and low temperatures limit the rate at which plant material decomposes.

In places the peat, or peat bogs, can be many metres deep. The lowest layers of peat can be thousands of years old while the top few centimetres may only be ten to twenty years old. This age variation is why peat is not technically a biomass. It takes too long to form and has to undergo a form of decomposition.

Peat preserves trapped plant remains, pollen, human artefacts and even bodies such as 'Pete Marsh', the 2300 year-old Lindow Man in Cheshire. To scientists these natural archives can reveal stories of past civilizations, botanical history and climate change.

Peat bogs also help to protect the Earth from global warming. As plants grow they absorb carbon dioxide. It is 'locked up' within the plant structure, and stored as the plants turn to peat. When peatlands are drained or disturbed however, the peat starts to decompose. The carbon dioxide is then released back into the atmosphere where it acts as a potent greenhouse gas.

Additionally, peat bogs can often ignite and burn on their own for long periods of time. In summer 2010 Moscow airport was closed and people had to wear masks against the smoke from uncontrolled burning peat bogs outside Moscow. There was disruption lasting over three weeks.

More than 20% of home heat in Ireland comes from peat and it is also used for fuel in Finland, Scotland, Germany, and Russia. Russia is the leading producer of peat at more than 90 million tonnes per year.

QUESTIONS

1 How is peat formed and why does it form well in Scotland?

2 Why does peat act as good preserver of plant and animal matter?

3 How does peat help maintain our environment?

4 📖 Investigate 'Pete Marsh' and write a paragraph on his discovery.

5 [calc] Look at the table of oil and gas consumption. Which three countries are the highest consumers? Which three countries are the lowest consumers?

6 List a few reasons as to why there is such a difference in the fuel consumption between these countries.

7 [calc] Use the information in this chapter to construct a bar chart comparing the oil consumption per person per year in the following countries: USA, India, Brazil, UK, China.

8 What type of biomass could Scotland usefully generate? Try and research anything we could grow and use as fuel.

GLOSSARY

Biomass A source of renewable energy

Commodity Something for which there is a demand (gas, oil, etc.)

Fermentation A chemical process which produces alcohol

Gigawatt Unit of power

Landfill A place where rubbish is deposited, a dump

National Grid Connection of power supply lines

PLANET EARTH
Processes of the planet

How gases behave

Level 3   What came before?

 SCN 3-05a

By contributing to experiments and investigations, I can develop my understanding of models of matter and can apply this to changes of state and the energy involved as they occur in nature.

Level 4   What is this chapter about?

 SCN 4-05a

I have developed my understanding of the kinetic model of a gas. I can describe the qualitative relationships between pressure, volume and temperature of gases.

How gases behave

In 1738 Daniel Bernoulli put forward the idea that **fluids** (gases and liquids) are composed of extremely small particles which are continually moving and colliding with each other. His idea was not accepted at the time as there was little experimental evidence to support it.

In 1827, a Scottish **botanist**, Robert Brown (1773–1858) was examining pollen grains and **spores** under a microscope. He noticed that the tiny pollen particles in the specimens were moving about in a strange, jittery way. He couldn't explain it at the time but did report his findings.

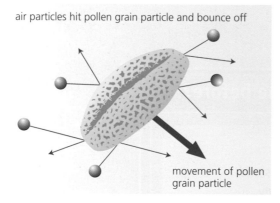

air particles hit pollen grain particle and bounce off

movement of pollen grain particle

These and other findings led scientists to believe that air (and all gases) is composed of tiny particles which are continually moving at high speeds. These particles are colliding with each other and with anything else (such as a tiny pollen grain) in their paths.

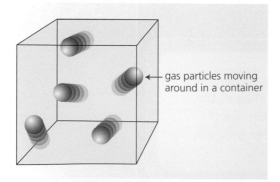

gas particles moving around in a container

The air particles that surround us are continually colliding with everything they come into contact with. The collisions are so small that you cannot detect them individually, but given there are billions of these particles around us their collective collisions can have an effect.

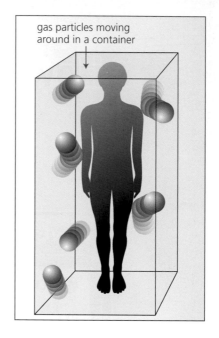

gas particles moving around in a container

Experiment

Your science teacher can do this experiment to show you the effect of these collisions.

Inflate a balloon and place it inside a glass container which can be evacuated.

Extremely small particles

When we remove the air from the container the balloon gets bigger!

The explanation for this is that there are now fewer air particles outside the balloon. With fewer air particles, there will be fewer collisions on the outside of the balloon. This allows the balloon to expand and get bigger.

We now allow some air back into the container.

More air particles now surround the balloon. This means more collisions and this results in the balloon being 'squeezed' back into its original size and shape.

A similar effect can also be seen in an aircraft. If you are given a pack of nuts or crisps when at high altitude you can see the bag seems ready to burst. This is because the pressure in the aircraft is not as high as when the aircraft is on the ground. This allows the air inside the bag to expand.

Don't open the packet but take it with you. Look at the packet when you leave and it will have the shape of a normal pack of nuts or crisps again.

Gas pressure

The effect of these particle collisions leads us to the concept of **pressure**. Pressure helps us describe the effect of these collisions on objects and to explain certain phenomena.

Pressure, and in particular air pressure, is the overall effect of all the little collisions that the air particles have on an object in contact with the air. Air pressure exerts force on us all the time but as

we grow up with this and are accustomed to the effects, we often don't recognise it.

Pressure and volume

Many things we use rely upon the effects of air pressure. The tyres on our cars and bicycles need to be inflated to the correct pressure so they work correctly. It's difficult to play football if the ball is at too high or too low a pressure.

How can we increase the pressure inside an object?

Take a football and a bicycle pump. To increase the pressure inside the ball, all we need to do is to pump more air into the ball.

Why does this increase the pressure?

The simple answer is that if we put more air into the ball this means the pressure inside the ball goes up.

A better scientific explanation is that when we pump more air into the ball there are now more particles inside it. Pressure is caused by particles colliding with the inside surface of the ball. As we pump more particles into the ball there will be more collisions and this will result in an increase in the pressure in the ball. The ball really doesn't increase in size much. Its volume remains fairly constant.

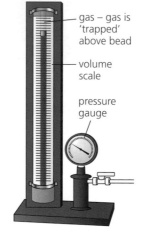

gas – gas is 'trapped' above bead

volume scale

pressure gauge

An Irish scientist, Robert Boyle, conducted a series of experiments where he measured the pressure and volume of a fixed amount of gas.

He took a measured volume of gas and measured its pressure. He then **compressed** the gas into a smaller measured volume and measured the pressure again. This procedure was repeated several times and he obtained a set of results for pressure and volume.

This graph shows that the pressure of the gas increases when it is compressed into a smaller volume. This result is known as Boyle's Law.

Can this law be explained in terms of particles and their movement and collisions?

If we have a fixed amount of gas it will contain a specific number of particles.

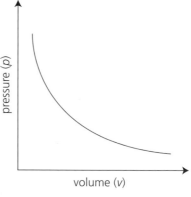

These particles continually vibrate and collide with the walls of the container. The collisions are responsible for the pressure of the gas. So if we reduce the volume the gas is contained within and we have the same number of particles, there will be more collisions with the container. This leads to the principle that the pressure of a gas increases when the volume is reduced. The opposite is also true. If we have a fixed amount of of gas and we increase its volume by expanding the volume of its container, then the pressure will decrease.

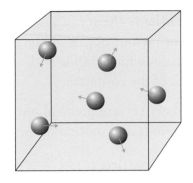

Pressure and temperature

Boyle was successful in his work on pressure and volume but he and other scientists were also experimenting to determine whether the temperature of the gas would have an effect on its pressure.

Experiments were performed with containers of gases which were then heated. In one experiment a container was sealed and connected to a pressure gauge.

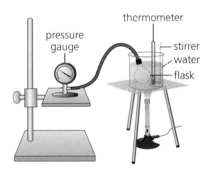

Such experiments showed that when the gas was heated its pressure increased, but this was dangerous. Some of the containers burst open when the pressure inside became so great.

This helps explain why buildings and cars sometimes suffer explosions during a fire. There are often sealed containers or cans that are trapped in the fire. As the fire progresses the temperatures in these containers or cans increases and this increases the pressure until the cans cannot contain it. When this occurs the contents of the cans explode or burst.

This too is why cans and aerosols have safety warnings about placing near fires or exposing to other sources of heat.

Can we explain the behaviour of the gas in similar terms to those for pressure and volume?

When we heat something we have to supply it with energy. If vibrating air particles are given more energy then they will vibrate and move more quickly. One way of thinking about this is to relate the temperature of a gas to the speed of its particles. The particles of a hot gas move more quickly than the particles of a colder gas.

Remember now that the pressure of a gas is due to the number of collisions the particles have with the walls of the container. If we increase the temperature the particles move more quickly. If they move more quickly they collide with the walls more often. This explains why the pressure increases when the temperature increases.

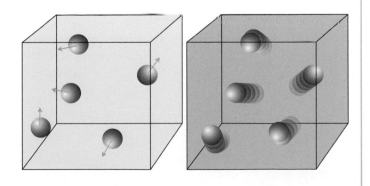

The kinetic theory of gases

The **kinetic theory** of gases attempts to explain the behaviour of gases in terms of their moving particles which collide with each other and the walls of the container.

It relates certain physical properties of gases to the behaviour and motion of the particles.

Temperature

This is a measure of the energy, in particular the kinetic or movement energy of the particles. High temperature means high energy so the particles move quickly.

Pressure

Pressure is caused by the collisions of the particles with the walls of the container. The greater the number of collisions, the higher the pressure.

Volume

This is the amount of space the particles occupy. We can change the volume a gas occupies by simply increasing or decreasing the size of the container. A gas will fit into whatever container we choose to place it in.

Applications of these principles

Inflating a tyre or a ball

We inflate a ball by pumping more air into it. More air particles in the ball mean more collisions by the particles on the inside of the ball so its pressure increases. We can detect this by feeling the ball become firmer and harder.

Breathing in

When you breathe in, your diaphragm (a lower abdomen muscle) pulls down and increases the volume of your lungs. This means the pressure inside the lungs reduces. If you then open your mouth, the air outside enters the lungs because it is at a higher pressure and it drives itself in. Breathing out is the reverse process.

Firing a bullet

A bullet can be broken down into a number of basic parts.

- The projectile part of the bullet.

- The casing or the cartridge of the bullet.

- The propellant which powers the bullet.

The casing of the bullet contains propellant or gunpowder. When the gun 'fires', this ignites the propellant. The powder turns into a gas at a very high temperature very quickly! The very rapid increase in temperature causes a very rapid increase in pressure. This gas at this very high pressure then pushes the projectile section of the bullet along the barrel and towards its target.

In old cannons a plug of cloth was forced into the barrel of the cannon to stop gases escaping at the side.

QUESTIONS

1 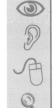 A pupil does an experiment where she measures the pressure and volume of a fixed amount of air. She then changes the volume and measures the pressure as she does so. Her results are in this table.

Pressure	100	120	150	170	200	250
Volume	50	42	33	29	25	20
P × V						

Copy and complete the table.

Using suitable scales, draw a graph of pressure (on the *y*-axis) against volume (on the *x*-axis).

2 In terms of particles, explain why the pressure in a tyre increases when we pump more air into it.

3 In the atmosphere, air pressure decreases as you go to higher altitudes and climbers at high altitudes struggle to breathe because the air is 'thinner'.

In an experiment a student releases a helium balloon and watches as it rises into the sky. After a while she sees it expand and eventually burst. Explain what she observed. Try to use terms such as pressure, particles etc.

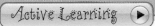

Activity

📖 In disaster movies we often see an aeroplane being damaged and the cabin losing pressure. This often involves objects being forced or blown out of the aeroplane by rushing air. Find out why this happens and write an explanation.

GLOSSARY

Botanist A person who studies plant life

Compress To squeeze together

Fluids Materials that can flow or move

Kinetic theory A way of describing the behaviour of gases

Pressure Force applied over an area

Spore A cell or structure that can reproduce

FORCES, ELECTRICITY AND WAVES

Forces

Float or sink?

Level 2   What came before?

 SCN 2-08b

By investigating floating and sinking of objects in water, I can apply my understanding of buoyancy to solve a practical challenge.

Level 4   What is this chapter about?

 SCN 4-08b

Through experimentation, I can explain floating and sinking in terms of the relative densities of different materials.

Float or sink?

You may well have been involved in a number of lessons in primary school and secondary school when you have investigated whether different materials will float or sink. In fact the Level 3 book in this series discusses the subject of floating and sinking and includes an extensive range of suggested activities. You could take some time to go back and read Chapter 11 on **Buoyancy**.

It's all about density!

The **density** of a substance is defined as its **mass per unit volume**.

That sounds a bit technical but it simply tells us that density is a measure of how many kilograms of matter there are in a volume of one cubic metre. Density is calculated from the formula

$$\text{density} = \frac{\text{mass}}{\text{volume}}$$

It's easy to remember what is meant by density if you memorise this formula.

Mass is measured in kilograms and volume is measured in cubic metres. Density is mass divided by volume and so is measured in **kilograms per cubic metre**. This unit can be abbreviated to kg/m^3 or $kg\,m^{-3}$.

It is usually quite easy to measure the density of a substance, particularly a solid or a liquid. All we need to do is to measure the mass of the substance and then measure its volume.

Why not begin investigating density by measuring the density of **water**?

Experiment: The density of water

1 Place an empty 100 ml measuring cylinder on an electronic balance and measure its mass.

2 Fill the measuring cylinder with 100 ml of water and measure the mass again.

3 Find the mass of the water by subtracting.

4 ⊞ Now calculate the density of water using the density formula.

Watch out! You must calculate the density in $kg\,m^{-3}$.

These conversion factors will help you:

- 1 kilogram = 1000 grams
- 1 ml = 1 cm^3 and 1 m^3 = 1 000 000 cm^3

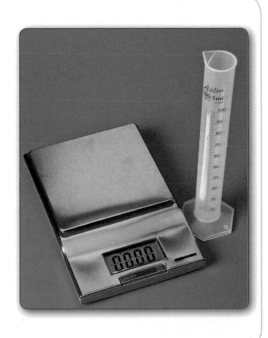

Experiment: The densities of metals

1 Your teacher can supply you with a selection of metal 'density cubes'.

Choose a cube and use a ruler to measure the length of its edge.

2 Calculate the volume of the cube in **cubic metres (m³)**.

3 Use an electronic balance to measure the mass of the cube and convert to **kilograms (kg)**.

4 Now calculate the density of the metal cube.

5 Repeat the procedure for all the metal cubes and record your results in a table.

The densities of solids and liquids

You would not be too keen to carry a large bottle of water, like the one shown, over a great distance. It is very heavy!

This is because water is a dense substance. Its density is $1000\,\text{kg}\,\text{m}^{-3}$.

This means that $1\,\text{m}^3$ of water has a mass of **1000 kg (which is 1 tonne!)**.

The reason that liquids, including water, are quite dense is because the molecules are packed closely together.

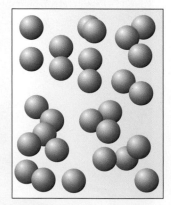

Molecules in a liquid are close together.

It is interesting to compare the density of water with the densities of solid metals. The densities of some metals are shown in the following table.

Metal	Density (in $\text{kg}\,\text{m}^{-3}$)
Aluminum	2768
Brass	8500
Iron	6975
Copper	8940
Gold	18 878
Lead	11 349
Nickel	8553
Silver	10 491
Steel	7861
Tin	7308

Experiment: The densities of metals

Look at the numbers in the table more closely. The metals are indeed denser than water but some not by as much as you might have thought.

The density of water can be written in **scientific notation** form as 1×10^3 kg m^{-3}.

If we do the same thing with the density of aluminium, we get approximately 2.8×10^3 kg m^{-3}.

The densities of some metals and water are not too different. They are in the same range (thousands of kg per m^3).

This is true for most of the metals in the table with the exception of the very dense metals lead, gold and silver.

What does this tell us?

It tells us that the densities of solids and liquids are **similar**. This indicates that the atoms or molecules in liquids are almost as closely packed as they are in solids.

Atoms in a solid are closely packed.

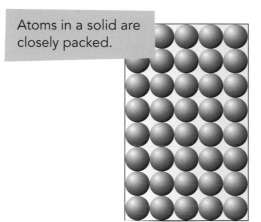

Experiment: The density of air

Your physics teacher can demonstrate how to measure the density of air by carrying out the following experimental procedure.

1 Measure the mass of a laboratory flask, fitted with rubber tubing and a valve.

2 Connect the rubber tubing to a vacuum pump and pump the air out of the flask.

3 Close the valve and measure the mass of the evacuated flask.

4 Calculate the mass of air by subtraction. (Mass of air = mass of flask and air – mass of flask.)

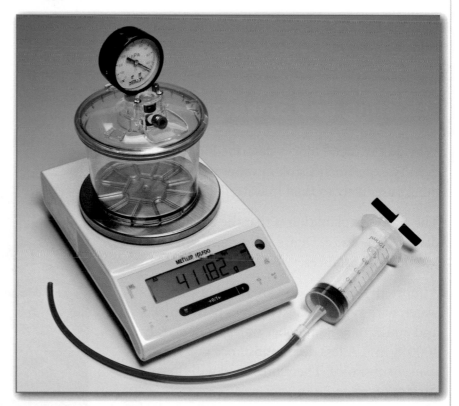

5   Place the flask in a basin of water and, keeping the rubber tubing under the water, open the valve. (A fountain of water will be forced into the flask by air pressure to fill the space previously occupied by the air.)

6   Use a measuring cylinder to measure the volume of water collected in the flask. (This is the volume of air evacuated.)

7   ☒ Calculate the density of the air using the density formula.

The density of a gas

The density of a gas can vary depending on its temperature and pressure. The previous chapter explained a little about how gases and the particles in gases behave under certain conditions.

Normally the density of the air in your school laboratory will be pretty close to a value of **1.20 kg m^{-3}**.

Carbon dioxide is denser than air with a density value of **1.8 kg m^{-3}**.

Helium is less dense than air with a density value of **0.17 kg m^{-3}**.

A careful look at these values reveals that gases are generally around **1000 times less dense** than solids and liquids. This is because molecules in a gas are **much** further apart than in solids or liquids. In fact, the average distance between molecules in the gaseous state is roughly **10 times greater** than the average separation of those in the solid or liquid states.

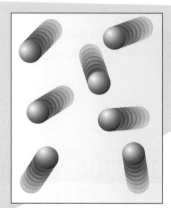

Molecules in a gas are widely spaced

Floating and Sinking!

Why do the metal blocks described in the previous density experiments sink in water while wooden blocks are likely to float in water?

The simple explanation is that the metals are denser than water. Dense substances will sink in less dense substances.

Almost all types of wood are less dense than water, with typical density values between 500 and 800 kg m^{-3}. Remember water has a density of 1000 kg m^{-3}. A less dense substance will float in a denser substance. Therefore wood will float on the surface of water.

⇨

a drifter!

Floating and Sinking!

Now we can explain why a helium-filled balloon will rise when released. The helium is trying to float to the surface of our atmosphere because it is less dense than air.

What do you think would happen to a carbon dioxide-filled balloon when released?

up, up and away!

Hot air

An **air-filled** balloon can also be made to rise in our atmosphere, just like a helium-filled balloon. All we need to do is heat the air inside the balloon. When a gas is heated it **expands**.

Expansion is the term we use in science when atoms or molecules move further apart. If molecules in hot air are further apart than in cooler air then hot air is less dense than cool air.

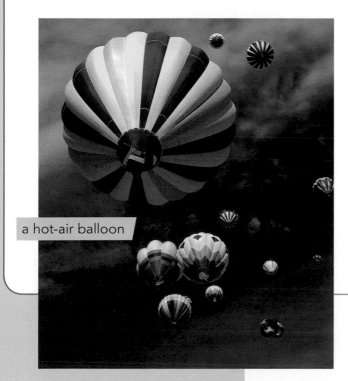

a hot-air balloon

To see how a hot-air balloon works you could use a Chinese lantern.

chinese lantern

However, you must be careful. You should only do this under the supervision of a responsible adult, and you should inform appropriate authorities, such as the Coastguard, if you are intending to launch lanterns. They could be mistaken for a distress signal! Chinese lanterns are amongst the most common items mistaken for UFOs!

Practical challenges

Now that you are clued up on the definition of density and how to measure it you can try the practical challenges below.

Practical challenge 1

Measurement of the density of a glass marble

Discuss with your classmates and your Science Teacher how to measure the density of a small object like a glass marble.

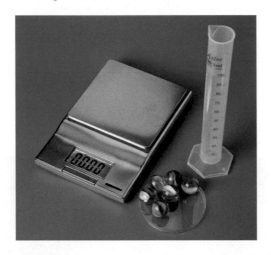

You are only allowed to use a 100 ml measuring cylinder and an electronic balance.

Practical challenge 2

Relative densities of different substances

This activity was described in the Level 3 book but it is worth re-visiting page 94 in Chapter 11 of that book because it is fun!

1   Use a glass jar or measuring cylinder for this investigation.

2   Collect different liquids which are **immiscible**.

(Immiscible means that the liquids won't mix with, or dissolve in, each other. Your Science Teacher, or someone at home, can provide a selection consisting of water, methylated spirits, thick syrup and cooking oil.)

3   Pour a quantity of each liquid into the glass jar and watch what happens.

4   List the liquids in order of *increasing* density. (That is least dense to most dense.)

5   Now add *small* objects such as a piece of rubber, wooden cork, marble, polystyrene sphere, plastic block and note where they go.

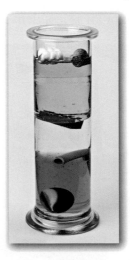

6   Now make up a final table, showing *all* the substances you have tested (solids and liquids) in order of increasing density.

Practical challenge 3

Density and concentration

We know that sea water (brine) is slightly denser than fresh water because of the presence of salt.

In Chapter 11 of the Level 3 book (page 91), it was explained how an egg could be floated in brine.

Make up a series of different concentrations of brine and find out what is the **minimum concentration** required to float an egg. (This can be done at home or in class.)

For example, if you add 2 g of salt to 100 ml of water then the concentration of the brine is

$\frac{2}{100}$ or 0.02 grams per millilitre. That is 0.02 g/ml.

Ships and submarines

If metals are denser than water how are we able to build steel ships which can float?

All ships, including metal ships, are able to float because of their shape.

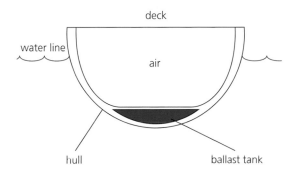

an aircraft carrier

The hull of a ship is not empty. It is filled mainly with air. The overall weight of the ship makes the hull sink into the water. As it sinks into the water it pushes aside (displaces) a large amount of water. The water in the sea 'pushes' back and it is this 'push' which keeps the ship afloat and makes the ship buoyant.

It is a serious problem when a ship develops a leak. Then water can enter the hull and replace the air. This means the ship becomes much heavier and can overcome the 'buoyancy' and sink.

How then does a submarine move to different depths at sea?

Submarines have to be built so that their overall density is roughly equal to that of the sea around them. They make use of large ballast tanks and compressed air.

In order to dive the ballast tanks are opened and sea water is allowed to enter. This water replaces the air in the tanks and makes the overall weight and density of the submarine greater. This allows it to dive.

In order to surface, compressed air is pumped in to the ballast tanks. This air forces out the water and makes the submarine lighter and less dense.

This allows the submarine to rise and surface.

time to abandon ship!

going down?

QUESTIONS

1 Write down the equation for calculating density.

2 In simple terms explain why a ball floats in water.

3 In simple terms explain why a piece of lead sinks to the bottom when placed in a basin of water.

4 Why do Chinese lanterns travel up through the air?

5 From the table of metals and their densities on page 26 list the five most dense metals and place them in order of decreasing density. (Start with the most dense metal.)

6 The *Dead Sea* is a sea in the Middle East. There is so much salt dissolved in it that the water is much more dense than tap water or sea water in and around Scotland. Do you think it would be easier to swim in the Dead Sea than in the sea around Scotland? Explain your answer.

GLOSSARY

Density The amount of mass in a unit of volume

Expand To increase in size

PLANET EARTH

Space

A short history of astronomy

Level 3   What came before?

 SCN 3-06a

By using my knowledge of our solar system and the basic needs of living things, I can produce a reasoned argument on the likelihood of life existing elsewhere in the universe.

Level 4   What is this chapter about?

 SCN 4-06a

By researching developments used to observe or explore space, I can illustrate how our knowledge of the universe has evolved over time.

A short history of astronomy

Astronomy not astrology

The study of our **Universe** is not a new science. The history of astronomy shows it to be the oldest science. People have been looking at the sky, amazed at its enormity and trying to explain what they saw, for as long as we can tell.

Early astronomers observed the sky and plotted the paths of the objects they saw. Their observations were used to try to determine certain events such as the longest day of the year, eclipses and the like. They also mapped the positions of objects and linked them to great events in the hope they could predict when these would re-occur. They believed the position of the stars and planets influenced the future.

This is what we now refer to as **astrology** but until the 16th or 17th centuries astrology and astronomy were considered the same science.

Astrology is not a science! It is a belief system based on the idea that the positions of distant **planets** and **stars** at certain times can influence man's future. It has no scientific basis however.

In early times however people were referred to as astronomers and/or astrologers and the observations they made were used for various purposes.

Even in early times special buildings were constructed for accurate observations so that readings could be taken and displayed in a way others could see. These buildings were called **planetariums**.

Ancient records appear to show that the first planetarium was built in China. The planetarium was a large enclosed dome-like structure with stars and constellations drawn on the inside surface. The person using the planetarium would sit in a chair that was hanging from the top of the enclosed dome. The purpose was to chart the stars and use them for astrological purposes. Eclipses and the appearance of stars and planets were thought of as significant. People placed great importance on these events and would wait for a sign from 'above' before taking important decisions.

These planetariums and other observatories were built around 2500–2300 BC. Observing total solar eclipses was a major element of forecasting the future health and successes of the Emperor, and **astrologers** were left with the difficult task of trying to anticipate when these events might occur. Failure to get the prediction right, in one recorded case in 2300 BC, resulted in the beheading of two astrologers!

Even 2000 years later in Republican Rome astronomical and other *auspices* (omens such as lightning flashes) were important indicators to the rulers and leaders. If seen as unlucky, the auspices could prevent Government business taking place on a particular day! William Shakespeare was aware of these Roman beliefs, as this quote shows.

'When beggars die there are no comets seen. The heavens themselves blaze forth the death of princes.'
Julius Caesar (II, ii, 30–31)

Predicting something like a solar eclipse is difficult and so it was a dangerous occupation being an **astronomer** in Roman times.

Progress in astronomy was being made however and Greek astronomers now noted that certain stars were relatively fixed in the sky while other bright objects seemed to move quickly in patterns different to the stars. These bright objects were called 'asteris planetei' or 'wandering stars'. These are what we refer to now as the planets.

$\Rightarrow$

Astronomy not astrology

Arab nations played a significant role in preserving scientific knowledge throughout the period 100 AD to 1000 AD. The caliph Al-Mansur (712–715), founder of Baghdad, started a programme to copy all surviving ancient Greek books and translate them into Arabic. This knowledge – the sum total of what the ancient world understood of astronomy, biology, mathematics, medicine and physics – remained unknown in Europe until mercenary knights defeated the Arab provinces in Spain. There is some evidence that Babylon had a number of **observatories** to chart the movement of stars and planets in some detail.

The motion of the stars and planets

The enormity of space

Before looking at historical interpretations of the **motions** of stars and planets, it is exciting to consider the sheer enormity of space.

Our Universe contains all matter and energy ever created and its size is difficult to comprehend.

Our **galaxy**, the 'Milky Way', has approximately 100 000 000 000 stars!

Our Universe however has of the order of 170 000 000 000 galaxies!

Our 'own' star, the Sun, is approximately 149 000 000 km, from us. Its light takes over 8 minutes to reach us.

The next nearest star, Proxima Centauri, is 3 970 000 000 000 km away! Its light takes over 4 years to reach us!

There are stars so far away that the number of zeros it would take to write down becomes impossible to comprehend.

Astronomy AD

People have attempted to understand and explain our place and position in the Universe ever since civilisations began to make records and diagrams. There are ancient drawings and carvings of the Sun and other stars which show people had been observing them and their movements.

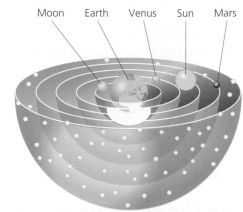

Moon   Earth   Venus   Sun   Mars

The early Greeks may have first suggested that the planets and stars orbited the Earth. That is, the Earth was the centre of the Universe and the bodies that orbited it were like objects caught in sort of transparent spheres. Spheres of different sizes were contained within each other, which allowed them to spin without colliding with each other. The furthest spheres held the stars. The Sun and the planets were closer. Beyond the stars were the Gods!

Claudius Ptolemy, in the 2nd century AD, suggested a slightly more complex model where the Sun, Moon, planets and stars all spin in slightly elliptic orbits around the Earth. He also gave indications of the speed of each of the main planets and the Moon. This allowed astronomers to predict when the various objects would be visible again. This theory worked reasonably well and was generally accepted for about the next 1400 years or so.

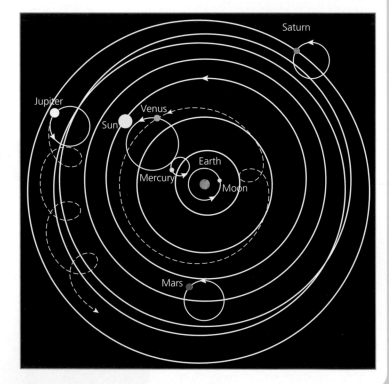

Closer observations by later astronomers began to find flaws in this theory and in 1540 AD Nicolaus Copernicus proposed a theory with the Sun at the centre of the Universe and the planets, moons and stars in orbit around the Sun.

Other astronomers such as Kepler, Brahe and Galileo were beginning to use telescopes and their observations gradually led to more sophisticated descriptions and explanations of the Universe.

The structure of the Universe

Sir Isaac Newton refined some of the ideas and proposals of the time and used his Theory of Gravitation to calculate accurately the orbits of planets, stars and moons.

Scientists were also considering how the Universe is structured, its size and how the stars are grouped.

Other interesting ideas and questions were being put forward about how many stars there are and how they are structured. It was suggested by some that there is an infinite number of stars surrounding us, but this idea seemed unlikely to the amateur German astronomer Heinrich Olbers.

Olbers' paradox (1823)

Olbers reasoned that if there is an infinite number of stars in the Universe and they send out light in all directions, then when we look at the night sky we should see it filled with *lots* and *lots* of dots of light. This should make the sky at night fairly bright since the light from all of the stars will reach Earth. Yet it is dark at night.

Why is this?

Any explanation of this is complex and there is some debate about what the true explanation might be. Answers include the fact that many stars are very far from us and are still moving away from us and the light from them has not reached us yet.

The Big Bang

Astronomers in the early 1900s noticed that the galaxies all appeared to be moving away from us. This led to a proposal by a Belgian, George Lemaitre, which suggested that the Universe was expanding and so all galaxies appear to be moving away from us (receding). Edwin Hubble expanded this and gave a greater foundation for Lemaitre's theory. Hubble found that all galaxies were moving and that distant galaxies were moving away more quickly than those closer to us.

An explanation was that an explosion must have occurred which blasted all the matter in the Universe in all directions.

Stars in the faster moving galaxies have travelled far and appear to be moving away from us. Stars in the galaxies which are moving slower than our galaxy appear to be receding from us.

$\Rightarrow$

The Big Bang

There was a lot of dispute about this theory and a British astronomer, Fred Hoyle, referred to it dismissively as some sort of **Big Bang** theory; the name has remained since.

Currently the Big Bang theory seems to explain a lot of what we have observed but there are still observations which are causing some problems. It seems well established that we live in an expanding Universe but this leads to other questions.

Will it expand forever?

Will it stop expanding?

Will it stop expanding and then contract?

It was suggested that the rate of expansion would gradually decrease because gravitational attraction between galaxies would gradually slow the rate at which they expanded.

The Hubble Space Telescope can look at the light from very distant galaxies and measure the rate at which they are expanding.

Since light from these galaxies takes billions of years to reach us, it is similar to looking at the Universe as it was all those billions of years ago.

It was expected that galaxies would be expanding at a greater rate then than now, since the effect of gravity on all galaxies (including more recent ones) would slow down the expansion.

Instead it has been found that the galaxies were expanding at a slower rate then than now!

The forces of darkness?

It appears that something has increased the rate of expansion.

Astronomers don't know what this is but have called it **dark energy**! It has an effect which we cannot understand or explain.

It gets worse.

We believe we might know how much dark energy there is because we can calculate how it seems to affect the expansion of the Universe.

It has been calculated that roughly 70% of the Universe is dark energy.

There is another mystery too. Astronomers think that there is a mysterious kind of **matter** that we cannot detect. This **dark matter** they think makes up about 25% of the entire Universe!

Everything else – on Earth, everything observed with our sophisicated telescope, all 'normal' matter in fact – adds up to less than 5% of the Universe!

So, in the entire Universe we believe that approximately 70% is dark energy, 25% is dark matter, and 5% is 'normal' atoms and matter.

This is difficult to believe but it's probably the best explanation of what we have now seen and measured with a wide range of telescopes.

Theories like these and their implications add to the impression that physics is a strange and difficult subject. These concepts are indeed difficult to understand but they arise from scientists' desires to explain what they see. The

The forces of darkness?

implications may be unusual but everyone can try to interpret them at their own level. This is in the nature of physics and its attraction for many people is the chance to explore and try to explain new and unusual things.

QUESTIONS

1. What is a planetarium?

2. Many early astronomers came from the Middle East, from places like Iraq and Iran. What is it about the climate of these countries that may have made astronomy such an important science in this region?

3. What did the ancient Greeks and Ptolomey believe about the structure of the solar system?

4. What do we believe now is the correct structure of the solar system?

GLOSSARY

Astrologer A person who studies astrology, which is the study of how the movement of the stars can affect human life (this is not a science)

Astronomy The study of stars and planets

Big Bang Term for a theory of the origin of the Universe

Dark energy An unknown type of energy which is present throughout the Universe

Dark matter An unknown type of matter which has been predicted to be present throughout the Universe

Galaxy A system of billions of stars with gas and dust held together by gravitational attaction

Paradox A statement of fact which seems self-contradictory or incorrect

Planet A large body (like Earth) moving in an elliptical orbit round a star (like the Sun)

Planetarium A building which shows stars and planets and their motions

Star A very large, hot luminous body in space, such as the Sun

Universe A very large collection of galaxies

FORCES, ELECTRICITY AND WAVES

Electricity

5

Electrical circuits

Level 3 What came before?

 SCN 3-09a

Having measured the current and voltage in series and parallel circuits, I can design a circuit to show the advantages of parallel circuits in an everyday application.

Level 4 What is this chapter about?

 SCN 4-09a

Through investigation, I understand the relationship between current, voltage and resistance. I can apply this knowledge to solve practical problems.

Electrical circuits

Electric current and voltage

In order to examine electrical circuits in detail we need to remind ourselves of the concepts of voltage and current.

Voltage is a measure of the energy being used by a **component** in a circuit. We measure the voltage across the component with a voltmeter.

Current is a measure of the amount of charge flowing through a circuit. Current is measured with an ammeter.

To investigate how voltage and current are related in a simple circuit, Georg Ohm built a circuit similar to the one below.

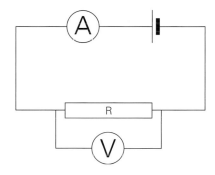

A sample set of results for such a circuit is shown in the table. The voltage (or potential difference) across a component is varied and the current through it is measured.

Voltage V (volts)	Current I (amps)
0.4	0.2
1.1	0.53
1.6	0.78
2.1	1.1
2.5	1.3
3	1.6

When a graph of these results is drawn, it appears as follows.

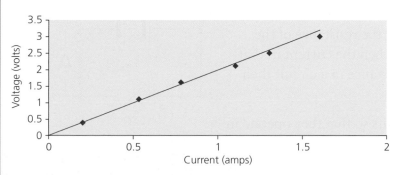

Resistance

The graph shows that if we increase the voltage across a component the current increases too. More than that, there is a link between the voltage and current. If we divide the voltage by the current we get a fairly constant answer. This constant (or ratio) of the voltage divided by current is called the **resistance** of the component. We can express this in an equation as follows.

$$\frac{\text{Voltage}}{\text{Current}} = \text{constant} = \text{Resistance} \quad \text{or} \quad R = \frac{V}{I}$$

The resistance of a material is a measure of how well it allows current to pass through it. Resistance is measured in ohms and has the symbol Ω (omega).

This result is known as Ohm's Law and it allows us to calculate voltage and current in simple circuits.

Exercise

Copy the table of results already given and add a third column headed $\frac{V}{I}$. Complete this column by calculating $\frac{V}{I}$ for each set of results.

Worked example

(i) A 6 V battery is connected to a bulb which has a resistance of $10\,\Omega$. Calculate the current in the circuit.

Now $R = \dfrac{V}{I}$ so $10 = \dfrac{6}{I}$. Hence $I = \dfrac{6}{10}$ or $I = 0.6$ A.

A current of 0.6 A would flow in this circuit.

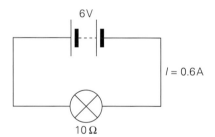

(ii) The $10\,\Omega$ bulb is replaced with a bulb of resistance $80\,\Omega$. Calculate the current in the circuit now.

Again $R = \dfrac{V}{I}$ so $80 = \dfrac{6}{I}$. Hence $I = \dfrac{6}{80}$ or $I = 0.075$ A.

The current is now 0.075 A.

These calculations show the effect of increasing the resistance of the circuit. If we have a high resistance in a circuit then the current in that circuit is low. Alternatively if we have a low resistance in a circuit then the current in that circuit will be high.

We use **resistors** to control the current in circuits so that they operate in the way we want them to.

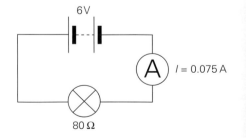

These images show resistors in a circuit and resistors that you buy in electronic stores. Resistors can range in value from low values such as 1 or 2 ohms to millions of ohms.

Resistance is a physical property of a material. It can be measured easily. It gives us information regarding atomic structure and we can classify materials depending on their resistances.

Conductors and insulators

Materials with low resistance are known as conductors. Metals are generally good electrical conductors and this is why the connectors in electronic components are made of metal and why house wiring uses copper wire.

Materials with high resistance are known as insulators and are generally non-metals such as rubber or plastic. These can have extremely high resistances and virtually 'stop' any current from flowing through them. This is why the outer sheath of cable or wire is made of plastic or rubber.

The best conductor of all is silver but due to its very high cost we use copper. Ultra-high pure copper is used for connecting very sophisticated hi-fi systems.

Some of the best insulators are those found on high voltage electrical transmission lines which can be seen around most areas.

Resistance in a series circuit

You should remember from your earlier work that there are simple rules to describe the voltage and current in a **series circuit**.

These are:

• the current is the same at all points in a series circuit

• the voltages across the components add up to a value equal to the supply voltage.

Using these rules we can analyse what happens when we have more than one resistor in a circuit.

Consider the following circuit.

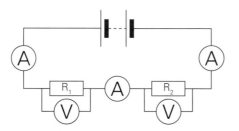

In the series circuit the current I is the same at all parts of the circuit. Using Ohm's Law we can calculate the voltage across each resistor using the equation $V = I \times R$. Voltage across R_1 is IR_1 and voltage across R_2 is IR_2.

Remember too that the voltage across each resistor adds up to equal the supply voltage.

So $V_{supply} = V_1 + V_2 = IR_1 + IR_2$.

The supply voltage (V_{supply}) can also be written as $I \times R_{total}$.

This gives $I \times R_{total} = I \times R_1 + I \times R_2$.

Since I is common to all terms we can divide throughout by I.

This gives $R_{total} = R_1 + R_2$.

This means we can calculate the combined or effective resistance of two (or more) resistors in series simply by adding them. This allows us to analyse more complex electrical circuits.

✕÷ Worked example

A 12 V battery is connected in series to a 50 Ω and a 250 Ω resistor.

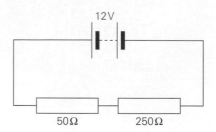

Calculate

   (a) the total resistance

   (b) the current in the circuit

   (c) the voltage across each resistor.

Solution.

   (a) $R_{tot} = R_1 + R_2 = 50 + 250 = 300$ ohms.

   (b) $I = \dfrac{V}{R_{tot}} = \dfrac{12}{300} = 0.04$ A.

   (c) To calculate the voltage across each resistor use Ohm's Law for each resistor.

     $V_1 = I R_1 = 0.04 \times 50 = 2$ V

     $V_2 = I R_2 = 0.04 \times 250 = 10$ V.

     (This gives a total voltage of 12 V which is equal to the supply voltage.)

✕÷ Worked example

A bulb and a resistor are connected in series with a 6 V battery. The current taken from the battery is 0.25 A and the bulb operates on 4 V.

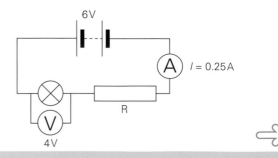

Resistance in a series circuit

Calculate

(a) the total resistance in the circuit

(b) the resistance of the bulb

(c) the resistance of the resistor.

Solution.

(a) $R_{tot} = \dfrac{V_{tot}}{I} = \dfrac{6}{0.25} = 24\,\Omega.$

(b) $R_{bulb} = \dfrac{V_{bulb}}{I} = \dfrac{4}{0.25} = 16\,\Omega.$

(c) voltage across resistor $R = 6\,V - 4\,V$
$$= 2\,V.$$

Hence $R = \dfrac{V}{I} = \dfrac{2}{0.25} = 8\,\Omega.$

Resistance in a parallel circuit

We can also connect resistors in *parallel*. This is a circuit which divides and in which the current can travel through either path.

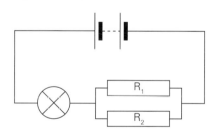

There are rules governing how the voltage and current operate in a **parallel circuit**. These are:

- The currents in the paths are independent of each other and can be combined to give the total current drawn from the supply.
$(I_{total} = I_1 + I_2 + ...)$

- The voltage across each path is the same.
$(V_{supply} = V_1 = V_2 = ...)$

These rules allow us to analyse the effect of combining resistors in parallel.

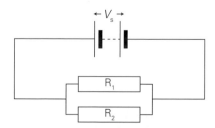

The best way to analyse this circuit is to consider the current in each of the resistors and then use Ohm's Law.

Now $I_1 = \dfrac{V_{sup}}{R_1}$, $I_2 = \dfrac{V_{sup}}{R_2}$. Since the total current is

$I_{tot} = I_1 + I_2$, then $I_{tot} = \dfrac{V_{sup}}{R_1} + \dfrac{V_{sup}}{R_2}.$

The total current is also $I_{tot} = \dfrac{V_{sup}}{R_{tot}}$

This means $\dfrac{V_{sup}}{R_{tot}} = \dfrac{V_{sup}}{R_1} + \dfrac{V_{sup}}{R_2}.$

Since V_{sup} is common to all the terms, we can divide by it throughout.

Hence $\dfrac{1}{R_{tot}} = \dfrac{1}{R_1} + \dfrac{1}{R_2}.$

This equation allows us to calculate the total resistance of resistors which have been connected in parallel.

Worked example

A 12 Ω resistor and a 24 Ω resistor are connected in parallel.
Calculate the combined resistance.

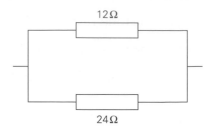

Solution

$$\frac{1}{R_{\text{tot}}} = \frac{1}{R_1} + \frac{1}{R_2} = \frac{1}{12} + \frac{1}{24} = \frac{2}{24} + \frac{1}{24} = \frac{3}{24} = \frac{1}{8}.$$

Hence $\dfrac{1}{R_{\text{tot}}} = \dfrac{1}{8}$ so $R_{\text{tot}} = 8\,\Omega$.

This method means that you have to be confident in calculations involving fractions.

We can do the same calculation but using the numbers with a calculator.

$$\frac{1}{R_{\text{tot}}} = \frac{1}{R_1} + \frac{1}{R_2} = \frac{1}{12} + \frac{1}{24} = 0.083 + 0.0417 = 0.1247.$$

So $\dfrac{1}{R_{\text{tot}}} = 0.1247$ and therefore $R_{\text{tot}} = \dfrac{1}{0.1247} = 8.02\,\Omega$.

This is not exactly the same as the earlier answer but it is acceptable.

An interesting point here is that when we combine resistors in parallel, the effective or combined resistance is always less than the resistance of the smaller resistor!

 Worked example

A 200 Ω and 50 Ω resistor are connected in parallel with a 6 V battery.

Calculate

    (a) the current drawn from the battery

    (b) the current in the 200 Ω resistor

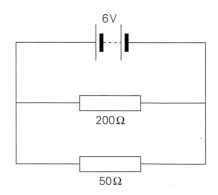

Solution

    (a) To calculate the current from the battery we need to calculate the total resistance of the circuit. So

$$\frac{1}{R_{\text{tot}}} = \frac{1}{R_1} + \frac{1}{R_2} = \frac{1}{200} + \frac{1}{50} = \frac{1}{200} + \frac{4}{200} = \frac{5}{200} = \frac{1}{40}.$$

        Since $\dfrac{1}{R_{\text{tot}}} = \dfrac{1}{40}$, $R_{\text{tot}} = 40\,\Omega$.

        Now $I = \dfrac{V}{R_{\text{tot}}} = \dfrac{6}{40} = 0.15$. The current from the battery is thus 0.15 A.

Resistance in a parallel circuit

Doing the calculation without using fractions gives

$$\frac{1}{R_{tot}} = \frac{1}{R_1} + \frac{1}{R_2} = \frac{1}{200} + \frac{1}{50} = 0.005 + 0.02 = 0.025.$$

So $\frac{1}{R_{tot}} = 0.025$ and therefore $R_{tot} = \frac{1}{0.025} = 40\,\Omega$.

(b) The current in the $200\,\Omega$ resistor is calculated using Ohm's Law.

Hence $I = \dfrac{V}{R} = \dfrac{6}{200} = 0.03$. The current is therefore 0.03 A.

Numeracy + − ÷ ×

1 Calculate the combined resistance of the following components:

a) $6\,\Omega$ and $10\,\Omega$ in series

b) $15\,\Omega$, $25\,\Omega$ and $40\,\Omega$ in series

c) $50\,\Omega$, $150\,\Omega$ and $15\,\Omega$ in series.

2 Calculate the combined resistance of:

a) $40\,\Omega$ and $40\,\Omega$ in parallel

b) $100\,\Omega$ and $100\,\Omega$ in parallel

c) $50\,\Omega$ and $50\,\Omega$ in parallel

d) $40\,\Omega$ and $10\,\Omega$ in parallel

e) $60\,\Omega$ and $20\,\Omega$ in parallel

f) $15\,\Omega$ and $10\,\Omega$ in parallel

g) $30\,\Omega$ and $20\,\Omega$ in parallel

h) $15\,\Omega$ and $10\,\Omega$ in parallel.

3 Simple lighting circuits in the home are examples of parallel circuits with switches in each section.

This lighting circuit is used in homes throughout the country. You can switch the lights on and off individually in different rooms.

Calculate the current in each room if the lights are all switched on. If all lights are switched on what is the current from the supply and in the circuit breaker?

Copy and complete this table:

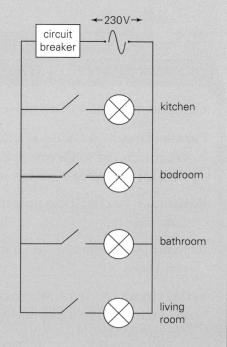

Room	Resistance of lights	Current used
Kitchen	150 ohms	
Bedroom	200 ohms	
Bathroom	250 ohms	
Living room	100 ohms	

Total current =

Domestic electricity

The circuit breaker

Occasionally a bulb will blow and have to be replaced. Sometimes when replacing it the circuit can be 'shorted'. This short circuit means a wire or a connector with a low resistance is somehow connected across the terminals of the bulb. Consider what would happen if one of the lights in the lighting circuit on page 47 was shorted by a wire of resistance $5\,\Omega$. This would cause a current whose value would be

$$I = \frac{V}{R} = \frac{230}{5} = 46\,\text{A}.$$

This is considerably more than the normal operating current and greater than the limit for the circuit breaker. It would cause the circuit breaker to trip and disconnect the circuit from the supply so that no one is injured. It would mean that the bulb would have to be replaced more carefully and the circuit breaker reset.

Household ring main circuit

In Britain, a ring main circuit is used to connect the sockets in rooms. This a form of parallel circuit which allows each plug socket to work independently of all others. It means we can connect and disconnect each plug without it interfering with other appliances in the room.

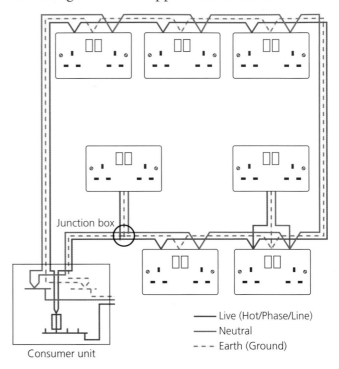

Junction box

Consumer unit

—— Live (Hot/Phase/Line)
—— Neutral
- - - Earth (Ground)

GLOSSARY

Component A part of an electrical circuit

Parallel circuit A circuit where components are connected so there is more than one path for the current to flow

Resistance An electrical property of a material

Resistor A component with a measured resistance

Series circuit A circuit where components are connected to make one path for the current to flow

FORCES, ELECTRICITY AND WAVES

Electricity

6

Electronic components

Level 4   What is this chapter about?

 SCN 4-09b

By contributing to investigations into the properties of a range of electronic components, I can select and use them as input and output devices in practical electronic circuits.

 SCN 4-09c

Using my knowledge of electronic components and switching devices, I can help to engineer an electronic system to provide a practical solution to a real life situation.

Electronic components

Electronic components are individual parts of larger pieces of electrical equipment. They are constructed to be connected to other electronic or electrical devices and are designed to operate in electrical circuits in particular ways. They can be simple components such as individual resistors or capacitors, or more complex (such as logic gates).

Electronic components can be combined to form electronic circuits which are then used to perform special actions or operations which we might choose.

Electronic circuits can be understood in a number of ways. The most common method of interpreting and understanding them is to 'break' them into different sections which perform different tasks.

We generally separate electronic components into input and output devices (amongst others).

Input devices translate some physical quantity into an electrical signal which can then be adapted in certain ways. An input device is generally the first section of an electronic circuit.

Output devices translate an electrical signal into a form we can use or react to. The output device is generally the final section of an electronic circuit.

Input devices

Here we look at some common input devices and how they operate.

1

This is the symbol for a **switch**. By pressing the switch a circuit is completed and an electrical signal is generated. This signal can then be 'processed' in some way.

2

This is the symbol for a **microphone**. A microphone converts a sound signal into an electrical signal. When sound energy is directed towards a microphone, a section of the microphone vibrates, converting the sound signal to an electrical signal.

3

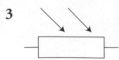

This is the symbol for a **light dependent resistor** (LDR). The resistance of the LDR depends on whether it is in a dark area or in a light area.

When light shines on the LDR its resistance is low. When the LDR is in the darkness, it has a high resistance. If the LDR is in an electrical circuit, any change in the light level will change the electrical signal in the circuit.

4

This is the symbol for a **thermistor**. The resistance of a thermistor changes when its temperature changes. When connected in a circuit this will change the electrical signal in that circuit whenever the temperature is altered.

5

This is the symbol for a **capacitor**. This device stores electrical charge. Electrons flow to and from its plates and gradually a voltage (or potential difference) builds up. The **time** it takes for the capacitor to charge up can be used in an electronic circuit. We might construct a circuit with a capacitor so that it sends an electrical signal when fully charged. A capacitor is useful in a circuit where a time delay is required.

Output devices

These electronic devices are found at the 'other end' of the system and in some regards they do the opposite of input devices.

1

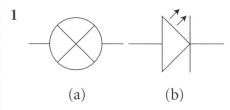

    (a)   (b)

These are the symbols for a **lamp** (a) and a **light emitting diode** (LED) (b).

These are devices which convert electrical signals to light. This might indicate to us that a switch has been pressed, or a signal has been counted, or a device has been switched on.

2

    (a)   (b)

These are the symbols for a **loudspeaker** (a) and a **buzzer** (b).

These devices convert electrical signals to sound. They can indicate for example when a process (using a timer) is complete by converting an electrical signal to an audio signal.

3

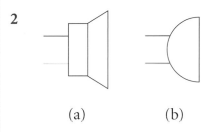

motor

solenoid

    (a)   (b)

These are the symbols for a **motor** (a) and a **solenoid** (b).

These are output devices which result in motion. Electrical signals sent to them are converted to some form of movement. A motor or fan can be turned on; a door or barrier can be raised. A solenoid is a magnetic 'switch' which can lock or unlock a door for example.

This method of looking at electronics in simple units is often referred to as a 'systems' approach. It doesn't deal exactly with what goes on inside various devices, but it enables us to consider the big ideas before analysing in more detail.

Electronic components

Active Learning ▶

The electronic components described on these pages can be used to construct some simple circuits to help us in our daily lives. We already use many of these circuits, often without realising that we are or we may have become so used to them that we take them for granted.

Electronic circuits contain a middle or 'process' series of components which takes the signal from the input device, processes it and uses it to control another device. For instance, the process section can act as a switch to switch on or switch off components.

Example

There are a lot of streetlights across the country and it would take a lot of switching to switch them on and off every morning and night. Instead they are controlled by automatic switches which turn them on and off at a certain times of day. Would it not be better just to switch them on when it gets dark?

We can design an electronic system to help us do this.

First of all we need an input device which responds to light. A light dependent resistor (LDR) would work here because its resistance changes when the light level changes.

We also need a switch and a light (in this case the streetlights).

LDR ⟶ switch ⟶ streetlights

The LDR is set to change when the light falls below a certain level. When this happens it sends a signal to the switch and the switch turns on the lights, so the lights are controlled by a switch.

Example

The thermostat in your oven acts in a similar way. We don't want the oven to get hotter and hotter so we use a temperature sensor – a thermistor. The thermistor is set to produce a signal when the temperature gets too high. This switches off the heater in the oven and the oven doesn't get too hot.

thermistor ⟶ switch ⟶ heater

The two sequences shown here have been simplified because there are a number of additional components needed for the circuit to operate but essentially this is how the circuits are designed.

Below are a list of sensors and a list of components. Show how you could use these items to design electronic systems to work in the examples on the opposite page. There may be more than one correct answer.

Sensors

Temperature sensor   Motion sensor

Water sensor   Light sensor

Thermistor   LDR   Microphone

Components

Alarm bell   Water pump   Lights

Motor   Solenoid   Heater

Fan   Buzzer

Examples

- A system to detect when a greenhouse becomes too warm and to water the plants in it.

- A system to detect when someone has entered a room and to lock any other doors in that room.

- A system that can detect too much sunlight entering a room and close the blinds.

- A system that can detect when a baby is making a noise and alert the parent.

- A system that can detect when a cat is coming back home and open the cat flap.

- A system that can detect a fire, warn people of the danger and try to put the fire out.

- A system that can open the garage doors when the owner's car approaches.

GLOSSARY

Component A part of an electrical circuit

Input device Something we use to send or control a signal to an electronic circuit

Output device Something we use to take some kind of information or signal from an electronic circuit

Resistor A component with a measured resistance

FORCES, ELECTRICITY AND WAVES

Vibrations and waves

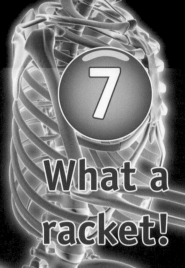

7

What a racket!

Level 2   What came before?

 SCN 2-11a

Through research on how animals communicate, I can explain how sound vibrations are carried by waves through air, water and other media.

Level 4   What is this chapter about?

 SCN 4-11a

By recording and analysing sound signals, I can describe how they can be manipulated and used in sound engineering.

What a racket!

Pollution?

A major problem in our modern world is that of **noise pollution**. This refers to noise levels which irritate us and can affect our general health.

The basis of the problem is the **loudness** of sounds. Loud sounds can have a harmful effect on our hearing and eardrums and lengthy exposure to constant noise can cause physical damage and also cause us to feel depressed.

Aeroplanes are a source of noise pollution

Turn down the volume!

We quite often use the word **volume** when we are thinking of the loudness of a sound. This isn't very scientific and might be confusing because the term 'volume' can also mean the amount of **space** occupied by an object.

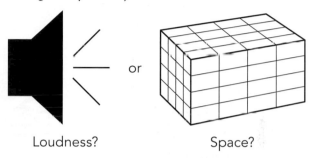

or

Loudness?   Space?

Sound engineers, like all scientists, measure physical quantities in special **units**. Each individual physical quantity has a unique unit. For example, distance is measured in metres, time in seconds and mass in kilograms. As you may know the unit which is used to measure volume is the cubic metre (m^3).

Sound level

Sound level is a physical quantity which can be measured and has its own special unit. The unit we use for measuring sound level, or loudness, is the **decibel** (dB). The measurement of sound level is performed with a **sound level meter**.

Sound level meters have built-in microphones which convert sound signals into electrical signals. The louder the sound, the greater is the signal produced. The meter then displays the electrical signal as a sound level reading.

Decibel scale

You may have noticed that the abbreviated unit for sound level includes a capital letter B. This is because the bel (B) (a very loud sound level) and the decibel (dB) were named in honour of Alexander Graham Bell who invented the telephone.

Alexander Graham Bell was born in Edinburgh, and from an early age showed great talent as an inventor. He emigrated from Scotland to Canada with his family where he worked as an engineer, scientist and inventor. Most of his work centred on human hearing and the science of sound. It is interesting to learn that both his mother and his wife were deaf.

The range of loudness of sounds is enormous. Our ears can detect very quiet sounds and also very loud sounds. This means that a simple measurement scale would need to have an extremely wide range. Engineers have devised a clever mathematical way of making sure that the sound level scale is easy to use without the need for extremely small or large numbers.

This scale means that an increase of 10 dB will make the sound level 10 times greater (more intense).

20 dB → 30 dB is 10× greater.

30 dB → 40 dB is 10× greater.

20 dB → 40 dB is 10×10× = 100× greater.

The scale is based on the formula $L_{dB} = 10 \log_{10}\left(\dfrac{I_1}{I_0}\right)$.

(I_1 is the intensity of the sound you are measuring and I_0 is the intensity at a reference point.)

Sound level

The decibel scale looks a little more user-friendly when you see it like this:

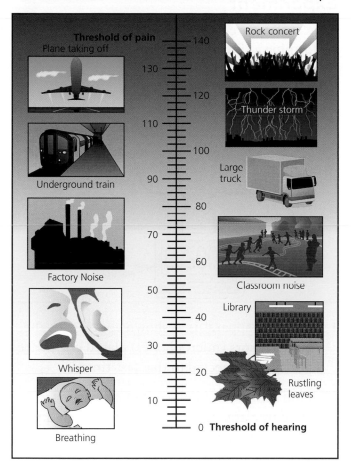

A sound level of 0 dB is the quietest sound which can be heard by a young human being without any background sound present. This is called the **threshold of hearing**.

Normal conversation has a sound level of about 60 dB and a rock concert can reach a level of about 140 dB close to the large speakers. Permanent damage can be done to our hearing if we are exposed to sound levels of 90 dB for lengthy periods of time. So, be careful when listening to music on your MP3 player. Turn down the volume!

The Noise Police!

The Physics Department in your school may be stocked with sound level meters. Ask your science teacher to show you how to use them. Then you can measure sound levels in different areas of the school, such as the games hall, the library or in a music room. Try measuring the sound level of the school bell at the end of a period … ouch!

Speed of sound

When you hear a sound, you are actually detecting a **wave motion** from some source such as a radio.

All sound waves are transmitted by the vibrations of particles (atoms or molecules). Energy is passed from particle to particle as the sound travels through a substance, or **medium**. When the particles in a medium are packed closely together it is easier for the vibration energy to be passed along.

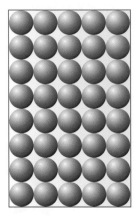

When particles are widely spaced however it is more difficult to pass the vibration energy along.

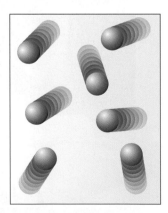

This explains why the speed of sound in most gases, like air, is slower than the speed of sound in solids and liquids. It also explains why sound waves cannot travel through Space. A vacuum has no particles to vibrate!

Experiment

You can measure the speed of sound in air by performing a simple experiment.

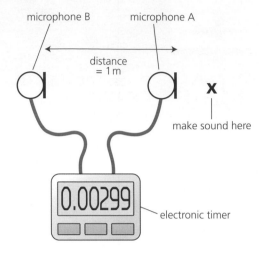

1   Set up the apparatus as shown above, with the sound sensors (microphones) placed one metre apart and connected to the 'fast-timer'.

2   Stand near microphone A and make a sharp sound by clapping your hands or tapping a glass bottle with a small hammer. (Be careful, don't smash the bottle!)

The sound wave will travel to (and beyond) microphone A which will send an electrical signal to the timer and start it timing. A very short time later the sound wave will reach microphone B (and beyond) and this will signal the timer to stop timing.

3   The speed of sound in air can now be calculated. (How?)

(Normally sound waves will travel through air at a speed of between $330 \, \text{m s}^{-1}$ and $340 \, \text{m s}^{-1}$. In water, sound waves will travel at a speed between $1500 \, \text{m s}^{-1}$ and $1600 \, \text{m s}^{-1}$. In solids, the speed of sound can range from $1600 \, \text{m s}^{-1}$ to about $2000 \, \text{m s}^{-1}$.)

Sound in a vacuum

The **space tube** is a piece of apparatus which can be used to demonstrate that sound cannot travel through a vacuum.

Switch on the buzzer inside the space tube, connect the space tube to a **vacuum pump** and pump the air out.

You should notice how the sound of the buzzer becomes quieter until you can hardly hear it at all.

Now switch off the pump and allow air to flow back into the space tube and listen to the buzzer getting louder again.

The science fiction film *Alien* used the slogan 'In space no one can hear you scream' on its advertising posters.

Seeing is believing

We are quite used to talking about 'sound waves' but seldom stop to think about how they might look if we could 'see' them.

We can listen to, and look at, sound waves if we connect a **signal generator** to a **loudspeaker** and a **cathode ray oscilloscope** (CRO).

1 Set the signal generator to produce a note from the loudspeaker and observe the **wave-trace** on the CRO.

2 Now increase the loudness of the sound and watch what happens to the wave-trace.

3 Next, set the loudness at a suitable fixed level and use the signal generator to raise the pitch, or **frequency**, of the note. Again watch what happens to the wave-trace.

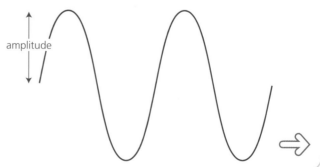

A loud sound possesses more **energy** than a quiet sound. The louder the sound the higher is the **amplitude** of the wave-trace observed on a CRO (see below).

The **frequency** of a sound wave tells us how many vibrations are occurring **every second**. For example, middle C, a note played on a piano, is generated by a piano string vibrating 256 times per second.

The unit of frequency is **hertz** (Hz). One vibration each second is written as 1 Hz. Thus, middle C has a frequency of 256 hertz (256 Hz).

Notice again that this unit, when abbreviated, is given a capital letter. This is because it is named after Heinrich Hertz, a famous German physicist.

A high frequency sound wave produces a high-pitched sound and will generate a lot of closely packed waves on a CRO trace.

A low frequency sound wave produces a low-pitched sound and will generate a few widely spaced waves on a CRO trace. Thus

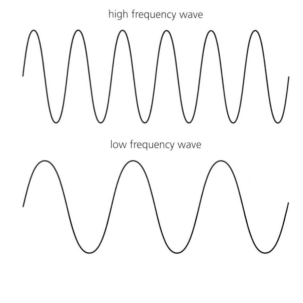

high frequency wave

low frequency wave

Music systems

In the last chapter we looked at 'input devices', one of which was the microphone. A microphone converts sound energy into electrical energy.

The electrical signal from the microphone can be stored on computer or magnetic tape. Once it has been stored we can play it again or manipulate (alter) the signal.

One simple alteration is to make the amplitude of the signal greater.

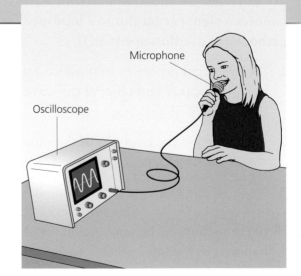

Microphone

Oscilloscope

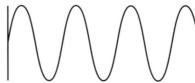

Increasing the amplitude is called amplification and this is essentially what the volume control does in an amplifier.

We can also amplify certain frequencies. For example lower frequencies in, say, the range 20 Hz –300 Hz.

This means the low notes are louder and give the sound a big booming 'feel'. For example drums and bass guitars produce low frequencies and their sounds are the ones which are amplified if you turn up the 'bass' volume. This can cause the room to reverberate a bit and can be heard easily in other rooms in the building. Good if you want to annoy the neighbours.

We can do the same for the higher frequencies and amplify them more than others.

This makes the higher notes louder and possibly clearer. It can also make the sound appear a bit light and 'tinny'. This is what the 'treble' volume control does.

When amplifying any electrical signal it is difficult to amplify all frequencies by the same amount. Most music systems are good for the middle range of frequencies but not across all frequencies.

Buying an amplifier that works well across all frequencies can be a very expensive business. High quality music systems can cost many thousands of pounds.

When we amplify a signal we might find the following.

It is difficult to take the input signal and amplify all of it perfectly. We often get little wobbles or kinks in the output signal. This is called 'noise' or 'distortion'. It is these little kinks which reduce the quality of the sound even though it may be difficult for you to detect.

Hi-fi is short for high fidelity. Fidelity means purity. So a high fidelity system takes a signal and increases it almost perfectly so that the amplified signal is a very pure version of the input signal.

People who over-enthuse about their hi-fi system are sometimes referred to as audiophiles.

QUESTIONS

1 What is meant by noise pollution?

2 List four things that contribute to noise pollution.

3 What is the unit of measurement for loudness?

4 List the loudness of the following noises:

   a) a normal conversation

   b) a rock concert

   c) the quietest sound we can hear

5 What is meant by the frequency of a sound?

GLOSSARY

Amplitude The 'height' of the trace of a wave

Decibel The unit for measuring loudness

Frequency The number of waves produced in one second

FORCES ELECTRICITY AND WAVES

Vibrations and waves

8

The wave nature of sound

Level 2 — What came before?

SCN 2-11a

Through research on how animals communicate, I can explain how sound vibrations are carried by waves through air, water and other media.

Level 4 — What is this chapter about?

SCN 4-11a

By recording and analysing sound signals, I can describe how they can be manipulated and used in sound engineering.

The wave nature of sound

If we were asked to draw a diagram of a sound wave we might draw something similar to the wave traces we have seen on a CRO. Thus:

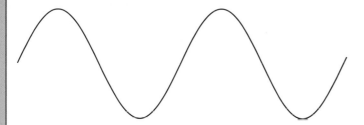

This type of wave is called a **transverse** wave.

A water wave is a transverse wave. Water particles bob up and down (in the vertical direction) but the wave energy travels horizontally.

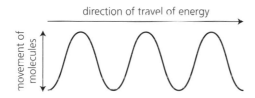

Sound waves are **not** transverse waves however, despite the fact that a CRO trace suggests they are.

A sound wave is actually produced by vibrations which move backwards and forwards in the **same direction** in which the energy travels. It is called a **longitudinal** wave.

The diagram below gives a better representation of a sound wave travelling through air.

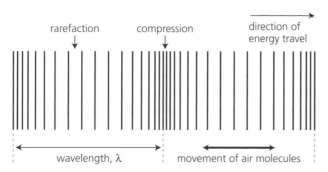

Your teacher can demonstrate both transverse waves and longitudinal waves using a slinky spring.

The diagrams below show the generation of transverse and longitudinal waves on a slinky spring.

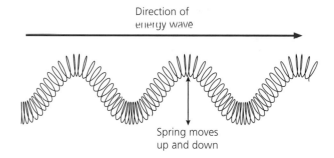

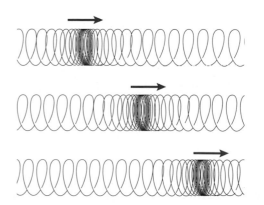

The wave nature of sound

Transverse or longitudinal?

So when we listen to sounds, the sound energy travels to our ears because air molecules (and in turn our ear-drums) vibrate **backwards and forwards**. The following diagram shows how we might picture this process.

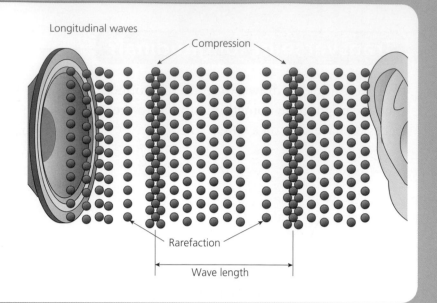

Longitudinal waves

Compression

Rarefaction

Wave length

When wave meets wave

A transverse wave consists of **crests and troughs** whilst a longitudinal wave consists of **compressions and rarefactions**.

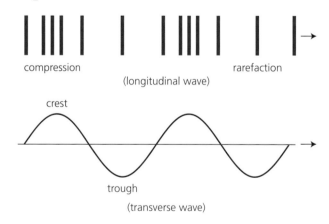

compression

rarefaction

(longitudinal wave)

crest

trough

(transverse wave)

When studying the behaviour of all kinds of waves however it is often convenient and simpler to think only in terms of 'crests' and 'troughs' as you will see in the next few paragraphs.

(It might help to think of compressions as being like crests and rarefactions as being like troughs.)

Waves often meet and pass through each other!

This is called **interference** and when it occurs surprising effects can be observed.

If waves from two sources meet and produce a wave of greater amplitude, we say that **constructive interference** has occurred.

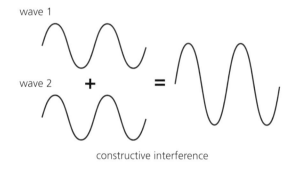

wave 1

wave 2

+

=

constructive interference

If waves from two sources meet and produce a wave of smaller, or zero amplitude, we say that **destructive interference** has occurred.

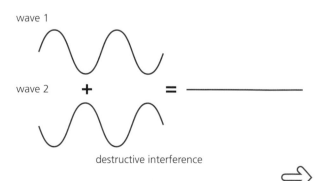

wave 1

wave 2

+

=

destructive interference

When wave meets wave

Although these diagrams illustrate interference with transverse waves you can investigate **interference of sound** by setting up an experiment like the one which follows.

Experiment

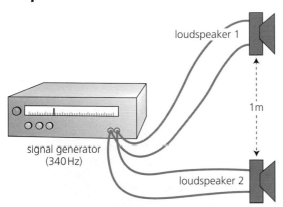

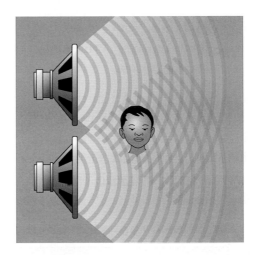

1 Connect two loudspeakers to a signal generator which is set at a frequency of about 340 Hz.

2 Place the loudspeakers about 1 metre apart and facing in the same direction.

3 Walk around the room in front of the loudspeakers and you will pass through regions of constructive interference where you will hear loud sounds, and regions of destructive interference where you will hear quiet sounds.

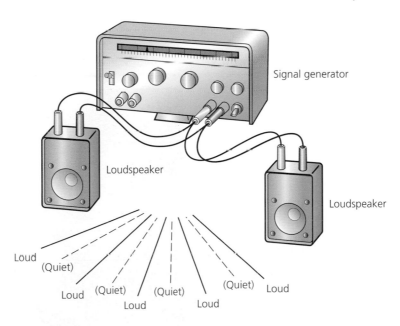

Noise cancellation – quieten down!

The idea of quiet zones where one sound cancels another sound out has led to a new type of headphone now available.

Noise-cancelling headphones reduce unwanted sounds using a technique known as **active noise control**.

In these, tiny microphones, placed near the ear, pick up any background noises and convert them into electrical signals. Special electronic circuits within the headphones then produce signals which are the 'mirror images' of the incoming background noise signals.

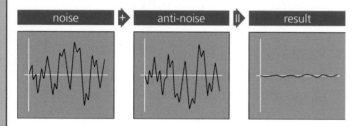

A 'mirror image' signal is known as **anti-noise** and is simply an inversion of the original noise signal. The noise and anti-noise signals combine by **destructive interference** and the unwanted sounds are therefore cancelled out inside the headphones.

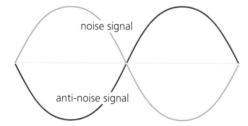

This makes it much easier for a listener to enjoy music without having to turn up the sound level too much.

Noise cancellation can also help a passenger listen to music or have a restful sleep in a noisy space such as an aeroplane. The headphones will cancel out the drone and hum from the aeroplane engines so it is like listening to music in a quiet room. They will also cancel out noise even when you are not listening to music. Switching on the noise cancelling button makes any room sound quieter.

relaxing music

zzzzzzzzzz...

Can you hear that?

Sound engineers are often concerned with **sound levels**. They also need to have an understanding of the effects of changing the **frequency** of sounds.

The human ear can hear a wide range of frequencies from approximately 20 Hz to 20 000 Hz. However sounds with frequencies greater than 20 000 Hz cannot be heard by humans, no matter how loud the sound. This is because our ear-drums are incapable of vibrating at such a high frequency and this results in very high frequency sounds being inaudible to us. Sound with a frequency greater than 20 000 Hz is known as **ultrasound**.

Some creatures, like chickens and frogs, are not able to hear over as wide a range of frequencies as humans. Other creatures such as bats, dolphins and dogs however can hear much higher frequency sounds than us. The scale of the chart has been adapted to allow the full range of frequencies to be seen.

'silent' dog whistle

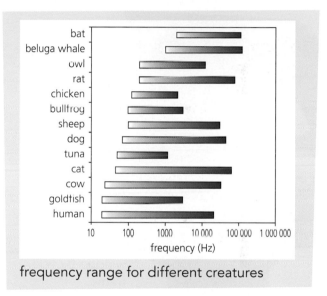

frequency range for different creatures

The sound of silence

Although we can't hear high frequency sounds, we can still make use of them. Engineers in industry have been using ultrasound for decades.

It is important that manufactured metal parts do not have flaws inside them. For example, the turbine blades in a jet engine have to be perfect, with absolutely no cracks. Surface cracks can be detected by visual examination but the detection of any tiny microscopic cracks **inside** the metal isn't so easy.

Engineers can detect cracks in welds for example, by using **radiography**. This involves 'looking inside' the metal using **X-rays** or **gamma rays**.

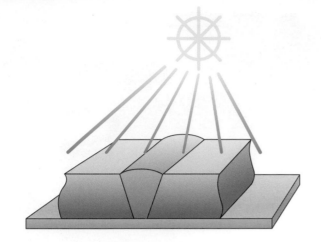

welded bicycle frame

Ultrasonic scanning is a cheaper and safer way of detecting flaws inside metal.

It can be done by sending pulses of ultrasound into the metal. The ultrasound is transmitted by a **transducer** probe which is placed on the surface of the metal.

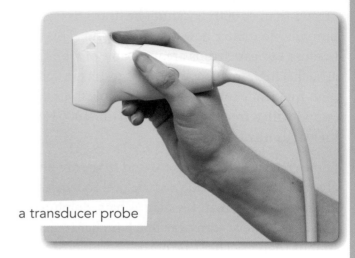

a transducer probe

The ultrasound waves travel at high speed from the transducer through the metal and if they meet an internal flaw, some of the sound energy is reflected back.

Experienced engineers can tell if a metal part is fit for purpose or must be scrapped.

The ultrasound waves do not damage human tissue and so there is no need for any expensive safety precautions.

However, there is a health risk associated with this kind of testing. Both X-rays and gamma rays (electromagnetic waves) are known as **ionising radiations** and they can damage healthy human tissue. This means that test engineers must take precautions such as wearing special protective clothing and carrying out the tests in special purpose-built rooms.

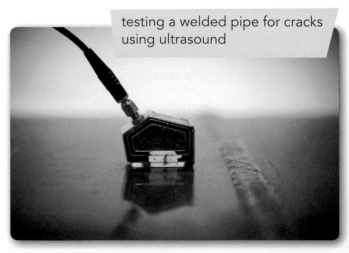

testing a welded pipe for cracks using ultrasound

Ultrasonics and medicine

Testing pieces of metal is one thing, but testing babies is another!

A Scottish physician, Ian Donald, proposed that ultrasonic sound waves could be used for some medical purposes. He realised that if it was possible to use ultrasound waves to find flaws inside pieces of metal, then the same principles might be applied to 'finding' an unborn baby in the mother's womb!

High frequency ultrasound waves can be transmitted from a transducer into the mother's womb. The waves travel through the womb which consists mainly of water. The waves reflect from the baby however and return as an echo to the transducer-receiver. The time taken for the echo to return allows a computer to calculate distance and so build up a picture of part of the baby in the womb.

For the computer to build up the picture, the doctor must **scan** the womb. This is done by moving the transducer across the mother's abdomen. The transducer head can rotate through a wide angle.

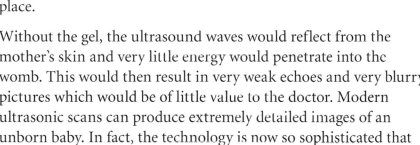

The mother's abdomen is smeared with a (very cold!) gel before the scan can take place.

Without the gel, the ultrasound waves would reflect from the mother's skin and very little energy would penetrate into the womb. This would then result in very weak echoes and very blurry pictures which would be of little value to the doctor. Modern ultrasonic scans can produce extremely detailed images of an unborn baby. In fact, the technology is now so sophisticated that detailed 3D pictures of the baby can be generated.

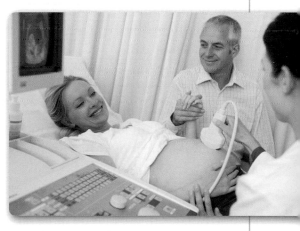

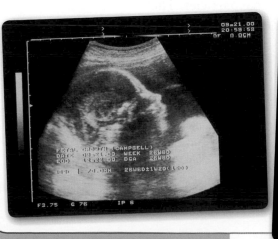

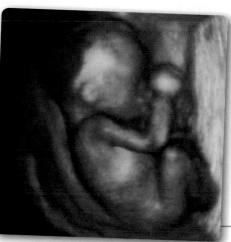

Kidney stones

Another very valuable medical application of ultrasound is in the removal of **kidney stones**.

kidney stones

Small hard crystals mainly composed of **calcium**, can grow in the kidneys and develop into small hard brittle stones. These can be caused by too much acid in the urine or a chemical imbalance due to eating certain foods. Sometimes a tendency to the development of kidney stones is a genetically inherited condition.

kidney stones form from crystals created by waste chemicals

kidney stone

ureter stone

Kidney stones cause a lot of pain and, if left untreated, can grow to be quite large. They can block the tubes which carry urine to the bladder and then make it very difficult to pass urine.

Doctors prefer not to operate on a patient to remove these stones because the surgical procedure is very delicate, complicated and recovery times can be long.

The preferred procedure is known as extracorporeal shock wave lithotripsy (ESWL). That is quite a mouthful!

In simple terms, doctors use X-ray photographs or ultrasonic scans to pin-point accurately the location of the stones in the kidney. A series of pulses of high-frequency ultrasound waves (or shock waves) is then directed into the kidney.

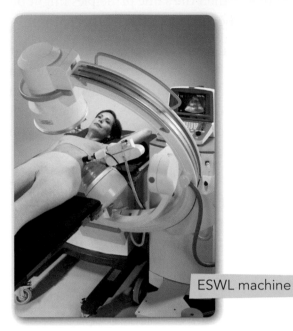
ESWL machine

The machine which transmits the ultrasonic waves usually has a large 'cushion' of water at the front. This is to ensure that all of the ultrasound energy is transferred efficiently to the kidney stones (rather like the gel used in a scan of a baby in the womb).

The brittle kidney stones vibrate and shatter under the action of the shock waves. The 'crushing' effect of the shock waves results in stones breaking up into sand-like particles. These tiny particles then pass out of the body naturally in the urine.

shock waves break the stone into pieces small enough to pass through the ureter

Shockwaves delivered through the skin

This procedure is almost painless and the patient can go home soon after having received treatment.

QUESTIONS

1 List the lowest and highest frequencies we can hear.

2 List three animals that can hear high frequencies.

3 List two animals that are able to hear lower frequencies.

4 List two medical uses of ultrasound.

5 ⊞ The graph below shows the frequency range of human hearing.

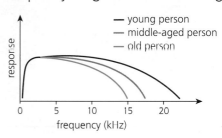

a) What range of frequencies can we 'hear' best?

b) At what frequency does each age group start to lose response?

GLOSSARY

Interference An effect that occurs when two or more waves meet

Longitudinal A type of wave transmitted by particles vibrating in the direction of energy flow

Radiography The use of radiation to view images of the internal structure of materials

Transverse A type of wave transmitted by particles vibrating at 90° to the direction of energy flow

Ultrasound Sound of frequency exceeding 20 000 Hz that is too high for us to hear

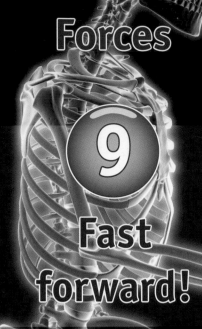

Forces

9

Fast forward!

Level 3   What came before?

 SCN 3-07a

By contributing to investigations of energy loss due to friction, I can suggest ways of improving the efficiency of moving systems.

Level 4   What is this chapter about?

 SCN 4-07a

I can use appropriate methods to measure, calculate and display graphically the speed of an object, and show how these methods can be used in a selected application.

 SCN 4-07b

By making accurate measurements of speed and acceleration, I can relate the motion of an object to the forces acting on it and apply this knowledge to transport safety.

Fast forward!

Distance, time and speed

Have you ever wondered how scientists figure out how fast something is moving? They can tell us some amazing facts, such as the **speed** of a fighter jet, the speed of electrons flowing along a wire in an electrical circuit, or the top speed of a cheetah when it is chasing an antelope for lunch!

Mostly, speeds are measured by doing experiments and using the very simple mathematical formula

$$\text{speed} = \frac{\text{distance}}{\text{time}}$$

Sometimes, speed cannot be measured by simply doing experiments alone, but also by performing clever calculations.

Either way, if an object is moving, a physicist will usually find a way of finding its speed, no matter how fast or how slow.

The formula indicates what normally needs to be measured for us to find a value for the speed of a moving object, namely **distance** and **time**.

Olympic track events

Consider a 100 metre sprint race. The simplest way to time such a race is to use a stopwatch.

Fast forward!

Olympic track events

The person timing the race must start the stopwatch when the starting pistol is fired then stop the stopwatch when a competitor crosses the finish line.

Can you think why this method is considered to be slightly unreliable?

A 100 metre sprint race lasts only about 10 seconds and so, at major events such as the Olympic Games, a more accurate method of timing is employed.

The athletes crouch with both feet on pads in the starting blocks.

The trigger of the starting gun is connected to a **timing console** (electronic timer) by long copper cables, and to small **loudspeakers** in each starting block.

When the timing official pulls the trigger, an electrical signal is sent to the timing console which then starts timing.

At exactly the same time, a similar electrical signal goes from the gun to the loudspeakers which reproduce the sound of the gun.

(The runners can quite easily hear the sound of the starting gun when the trigger is pulled. So why is it necessary to have loudspeakers at each starting block?)

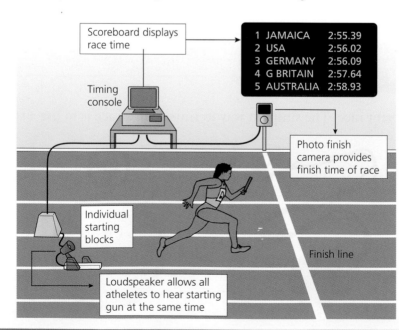

Scoreboard displays race time

1	JAMAICA	2:55.39
2	USA	2:56.02
3	GERMANY	2:56.09
4	G BRITAIN	2:57.64
5	AUSTRALIA	2:58.93

Timing console

Photo finish camera provides finish time of race

Individual starting blocks

Finish line

Loudspeaker allows all atheletes to hear starting gun at the same time

Olympic track events

A photo-finish camera is placed at the finishing line to help officials decide the winner in a close finish. This camera can take 1000 pictures per second!

However, the actual timing of the runners is completed by means of a **laser beam** directed along the finishing line and aimed directly at a **light sensor**. When a runner crosses the finishing line the laser beam is blocked and the light sensor sends another electrical signal to the timing console. This signal causes the console to stop timing.

Advanced timing technology like this can measure a sprinter's time to within $\frac{1}{1000}$ second which is $\frac{1}{40}$ of the time it takes you to blink an eye! This very short time interval can make the difference between gold and silver!

Experiment 1

Electronic timing

You can set up your own 'timing console' to measure a time interval and then calculate the speed of a vehicle. Your teacher will assist you with setting up the apparatus.

You need:

- an air-track and air-track vehicle (called a 'glider') fitted with a card, or 'mask', as shown

- an electronic timer which is capable of being triggered by two 'light-gates' (light beams and sensors)

- two light-gates and two clamp stands

- a metre stick.

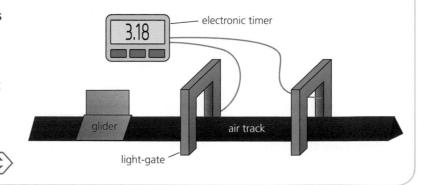

Experiment 1

What to do:

1 Programme the electronic timer to **triggered mode**.

2 Set up the apparatus as shown taking care to check that the air-track is absolutely level.

3 Place the two light-gates over the track and use the metre stick to position them a measured distance apart (40 cm or 50 cm say).

4 Make sure that the glider and card move through the light-gates so that the card 'cuts' each of the beams.

5 Gently push the glider from one end of the track so that it glides along slowly.

(When the glider passes through the first light-gate, the card 'cuts' the first beam and the electronic timer starts timing. When the glider passes through the second light-gate, the card 'cuts' the second beam and stops the timer.)

6 ⊞ You can now calculate the **average speed** of the glider as it travelled between the two light-gates by using the speed formula given earlier. Your final result should be quoted in **metres per second** (m s^{-1}).

7 Repeat the experiment for different speeds.

Make use of the technology!

This last experiment requires *you* to calculate speed from measurements of distance and time.

Computers however are quite capable of doing the calculation for us. It is easy to programme a small computer-like device to capture experimental data and display a value for speed immediately.

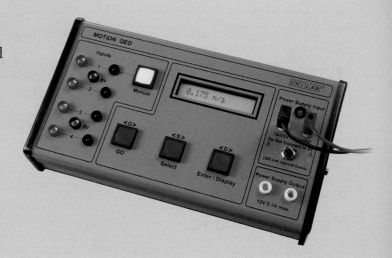

Experiment 2

Electronic measurement of speed

Now try this investigation using a device such as the one shown in the last photograph. (Your school may have a different model, but the basic use and operation will be the same.)

1 Set up an air-track and glider, or a ramp and dynamics trolley. The air-track or ramp should be inclined so that the vehicle will speed up as it moves down the slope as shown. This speeding up is called **acceleration**.

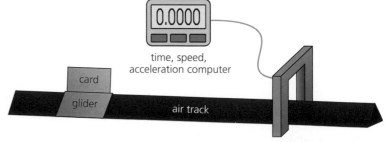

2   Measure the length of the card attached to the vehicle.

3   Programme the time/speed/acceleration computer to measure speed. (Your teacher can show you how to do this.)

4   Place a light-gate near the top of the slope so that the card will cut the beam when the vehicle passes through.

5   Allow the vehicle to start from rest at the top of the slope and pass through the light-gate.

6   Record the speed displayed by the mini-computer.

7   Move the light-gate to the middle of the slope and repeat.

8   Now move the light-gate to near the bottom of the slope and repeat.

Average or instantaneous?

Experiment 1 used **two** light-gates because the task was to measure the time taken for the glider to move from one point on the track to another. This led to the calculation of the glider's **average speed**. The formula used to do this is

$$\text{average speed} = \frac{\text{total distance travelled}}{\text{total time taken}}$$

Experiment 2 used only **one** light gate. This was because a computer was able to measure the time taken by the card to cut the beam. The computer then calculated the speed as it passed through the light gate.

This is known as the **instantaneous speed**.

The formula used by the computer to calculate instantaneous speed is

$$\text{instantaneous speed} = \frac{\text{length of card}}{\text{time for card to cut beam}}$$

A motorist must know the actual speed of his or her car at any instant during a journey. The **speedometer** on the dashboard indicates the instantaneous speed of the car.

On some roads where there have been a high number of accidents, **average speed cameras** are positioned a known distance apart.

The time taken for a car to move from one camera to the next is timed electronically and a computer calculates the average speed. Drivers who exceed the permitted average speed usually receive a hefty fine!

Traffic police use a variety of methods of measuring the speeds of motor cars in the interests of public safety. Their use of speed cameras is explained in more detail at:

www.lordpercy.com/speed_cameras_explained.htm

Use the technology!

The following link allows you to download your very own speedometer as an 'app' on your mobile phone:

www.mobiletopsoft.com/board/5530/measure-your-speed-with-gps-speedometer.html

The next link allows you to download a free 'speedometer app' for your iPad. You can use it to measure your speed if you are travelling on a car, train, boat or plane, or simply walking along the street! It is:

www.mbtheme.com/ipad_apps/entertainment/Speedometer--Digital---Analog-And-Free-_64063-64063.html

Acceleration and deceleration

By now you should know how to measure speeds and how to calculate the speeds of moving objects.

However, it is important to realise that an object such as a car cannot achieve a particular speed unless it has been 'speeded up' from a lower speed or from rest. This requires an accelerating **force** to be applied to the car by its engine.

Conversely, a car travelling at a high speed can only slow down or come to a halt, if a decelerating force is applied to the car by its brakes.

The acceleration (or deceleration) of any moving object can be calculated or measured quite easily. However, you have to understand that **acceleration** is not the same as **speed**.

Acceleration is a measure of how quickly a moving object can **increase** its speed.

Deceleration is a measure of how quickly a moving object can **decrease** its speed.

What a performance!

To help you better understand this, consider the following data for two cars.

Initial speed = 0 metres per second (m s⁻¹)	Initial speed = 0 metres per second (m s⁻¹)
final speed = 28 m s⁻¹	final speed = 28 m s⁻¹
time taken to change speed = 13 seconds	time taken to change speed = 4 seconds

Acceleration and deceleration

It is obvious that the car on the right can achieve a high speed from a 'standing start' in a much shorter time than the car on the left. This is called the **performance** of the car, but we should recognise it as the **acceleration** of the car.

A value for the acceleration of each car can be calculated from the data by using a fairly simple formula:

$$\text{acceleration} = \frac{\text{change in speed}}{\text{time taken to change speed}}$$

So now for some maths!

Acceleration $= \dfrac{28 - 0}{13}$ $\qquad$ Acceleration $= \dfrac{28 - 0}{4}$

$\qquad\qquad\quad = \dfrac{28}{13}$ $\qquad\qquad\qquad\quad = \dfrac{28}{4}$

$\qquad\qquad\quad = 2.15\,\text{m s}^{-2}$ $\qquad\qquad\quad = 7\,\text{m s}^{-2}$

Did you notice the strange unit (m s^{-2}) in both answers? What does it mean?

The calculation for the first car tells us that when its maximum engine force is applied, the car is capable of increasing its speed by 2.15 metres per second **every second**. This is the acceleration of the car.

Compare this value with that of the second car. When its engine applies maximum force, it can increase its speed by 7 metres per second **every second**. This is a much greater acceleration.

So the strange unit m s^{-2} is an abbreviation for **'metres per second per second'**. This is the unit which we use for acceleration.

The formula for acceleration can be written in a more convenient mathematical form. This is:

$$a = \frac{v - u}{t}$$

where $\quad a = $ acceleration (m s^{-2})
$\qquad\quad v = $ final speed (m s^{-1})
$\qquad\quad u = $ initial speed (m s^{-1})
$\qquad\quad t = $ time taken to change speed (s).

Measuring acceleration

By now you should have used an electronic 'mini-computer' and light gate to measure **instantaneous speed**.

To measure the **acceleration** of a dynamics trolley or an air-track glider however, we need to measure **two** instantaneous speeds (initial and final) and the time taken **between** these two speeds.

This can be done easily provided you prepare a card (or mask) which is correctly shaped to do the job. The shape required is like the one below.

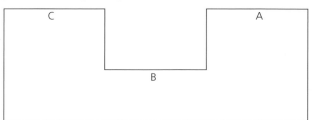

Measuring acceleration

We cut the mask from card so that each section, A, B and C, of the mask is the same width (say 2 cm) and then attach it to the vehicle.

Your teacher will show you how to programme the mini-computer to measure acceleration. The experiment is then conducted as follows.

1   Set up an incline. In other words tilt your ramp or air track so that the vehicle will speed up as it travels down the slope.

2   When the vehicle or glider passes through the light gate, the mini-computer will measure the time taken by section A of the mask to cut the beam and then calculate an initial instantaneous speed. The time taken for section C of the mask to cut the beam allows the mini-computer to calculate a final instantaneous speed.

3   The computer will then compute and display the acceleration of the vehicle.

What is the purpose of section B of the mask? Discuss with your classmates and/or your teacher.

Investigating acceleration and force

Here is an experimental investigation which will allow you to produce data for an air track glider which is accelerating due to an applied accelerating force. The data you produce will enable you to draw a graph of the acceleration against the accelerating force. (The accelerating force is often referred to as the unbalanced force.)

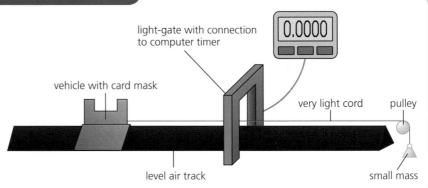

light-gate with connection to computer timer

0.0000

vehicle with card mask

very light cord   pulley

level air track

small mass

1   Set up the apparatus as shown.

2   Tie a small mass, say 10 g, to the light cord which is connected to the vehicle and passes over a pulley.

(Since there is little or no friction on the air track, the weight of this mass becomes the accelerating force.)

3   Release the vehicle and record the acceleration as it passes through the light-gate.

4   Add another 10 g mass and repeat.

5   Record results for 10 g, 20 g, 30 g and 40 g.

6   🔢 Plot a graph of **force** on the x-axis against **acceleration** on the y-axis.

(Be careful however. The **force** which accelerates the vehicle is the **weight** of the mass attached to the cord. Check with your teacher or look back to Book 3 (p. 82) before you convert mass to weight.)

What does your graph look like?

What does this suggest about acceleration and force?

Force and motion

Experiments like this help us understand the link between acceleration and force.

This link was first investigated by Sir Isaac Newton.

Newton was a very clever physicist and mathematician who realised that when a mass is acted upon by a set of **balanced forces** or zero force, then the mass will either stay at rest or travel at constant speed. This was the basis of **Newton's first law of motion**.

The consequences of this law can be seen in car crashes.

Drivers and passengers who are foolish enough to travel without wearing seatbelts may discover that Newton's first law of motion can spell danger!

The lamp post exerted a decelerating force on this car and brought it to a halt. However, any occupants who were not wearing seat-belts would have no forces acting on them and would continue to move forward inside the car until they collided with the windscreen!

Follow this link to read about Newton's first law of motion in more detail:

www.physicsclassroom.com/Class/newtlaws/u2l1a.html

Seat belts offer protection from injury by exerting a restraining **decelerating force** in the direction opposite to the forward motion of the driver or passenger, and so bring him or her safely to a halt.

The occupant of the car is obeying **Newton's second law of motion** which predicts that an **unbalanced force** will cause an object either to accelerate or decelerate.

You may remember from Book 3 that we wrote this law as $F_{un} = ma$.

An air bag does a similar job and stops the driver's head or passenger's head colliding with the steering wheel or dashboard.

Force and motion

Numeracy + − ÷ ×

The following speed-time graphs show how the speed of a 50 kg man varies from the instant his car travelling at $15\,m\,s^{-1}$, collides with a wall.

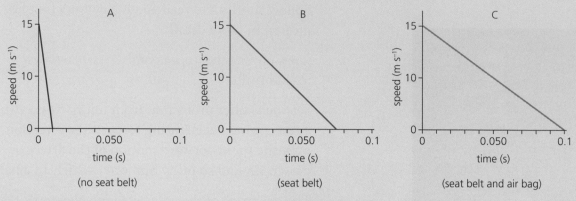

A (no seat belt)

B (seat belt)

C (seat belt and air bag)

Graph A is for a driver who is not wearing a seat belt.

Graph B is for a driver who is wearing a seat belt.

Graph C is for a driver who is wearing a seat belt and is driving a car fitted with an air bag.

1 Use the formula $a = \dfrac{v-u}{t}$ to calculate the deceleration (negative acceleration) of the driver in each case.

2 Use the formula $F_{un} = ma$ to calculate the decelerating force in each case.

3 What force caused the driver to slow down in Graph A?

(Look back to Chapter 8 in the Level 3 book for more practice questions using the equation $F_{un} = ma$.)

Full of bounce!

Perhaps the most spectacular use of airbags can be seen in NASA's **Pathfinder Mission** to Mars.

The Pathfinder rocket was launched in 1996 and took 7 months to reach Mars. The mission was to carry out chemical analysis of the rocky material on the surface of the planet and send data back to Earth, including photographs.

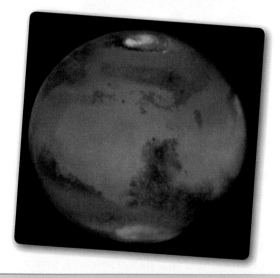

Full of bounce!

Rock sampling and chemical analysis was to be carried out by a roving solar-powered vehicle called the **Sojourner**.

Chemical analysis results from the Sojourner, and photographs, were to be transmitted back to Earth by solar-powered radios and cameras.

This expensive equipment had to be landed safely on Mars remotely. (Mankind hasn't travelled to Mars yet but it may happen in your lifetime!)

The **landing capsule** could have been slowed down and landed using **retro-rockets**. However chemicals from the burnt fuel might have contaminated the rock samples and spoiled the results of chemical analysis.

The NASA engineers and scientists decided therefore to use a combination of retro-rockets and a parachute to slow the vehicle down from an approach speed of 17 000 mph in Space to between 50 mph and 60 mph in Mars's atmosphere. Therefore the capsule had to be allowed to strike the surface of Mars at a speed of about 50 mph! This is similar to a very serious car crash! The engineers elected to use the same technology which car manufacturers used to protect drivers and passengers, namely, the air bag.

The contents of the landing capsule were protected by a pyramid-shaped structure composed of 24 air bags. When it collided with the surface it literally bounced along until it eventually came to a halt.

Thereafter the air bags deflated automatically, solar cells opened up like the petals of a flower and the rover vehicle ventured out onto the surface of Mars to start work!

To obtain more detail on this amazing landing procedure, follow the link below.

http://science.jrank.org/pages/4148/Mars-Pathfinder.html

QUESTIONS

1 State the formula for calculating speed.

2  A sprinter completes a 100 m race in 12.5 seconds. Calculate the average speed of the sprinter in m s^{-1}. What is this speed in km h^{-1}?

3   A 1500 m runner completes the race in 3 minutes 30 seconds. Calculate her average speed.

4 A 10000 m runner completes the race in 30 minutes 50 seconds. Calculate the average speed of the runner.

5 Why are electronic timing devices used to measure the speeds of runners in important races?

6 Many roads use 'average speed cameras' to deter drivers from speeding. Write a paragraph to describe how these cameras work.

7 'Acceleration' is a term used when describing the performance of some cars. Describe in simple terms what 'acceleration' means.

8 Cars involved in crashes now are safer statistically than 10 years ago. This means that if you are involved in a collision your chances of survival are much better. List two developments in modern cars which have made this possible.

Active Learning ▶

Cars should be designed to travel safely and legally at speeds over 100 mph.

Write a small report saying why you agree or disagree with this statement.

GLOSSARY

Acceleration How quickly speed changes

Average speed The speed of an object over a measured distance

Force Something that can change the speed, shape or direction of an object

Instantaneous speed The speed of an object at a particular instant

Speed The distance in metres covered by an object in one second

FORCES, ELECTRICITY AND WAVES

Forces

10

What's the attraction?

Level 2 — What came before?

 SCN 2-08a

I have collaborated in investigations to compare magnetic, electrostatic and gravitational forces and have explored their practical applications.

Level 4 — What is this chapter about?

 SCN 4-08a

I can help to design and carry out investigations into the strength of magnets and electromagnets. From investigations, I can compare the properties, uses and commercial applications of electromagnets and supermagnets.

What's the attraction?

Magnetic fields

Most of us have played with magnets at some time. We are intrigued by them and usually fascinated by their ability to **attract** some metals, and each other, often with quite a big pulling force.

Magnets come in many different shapes and sizes. The most common types of magnet are the **bar magnet** and the **horseshoe magnet**. (The horseshoe magnet is simply a bar magnet which is bent into a curve the shape of a horseshoe.) These magnets are called **permanent** magnets.

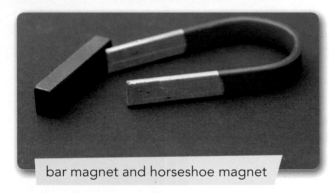

bar magnet and horseshoe magnet

All magnets have a **north pole** and a **south pole**. A bar magnet has its poles at the ends.

All magnets have an invisible **force field** surrounding them.

The magnet's force field can attract some metals towards the magnet. It can also push other magnets away or pull them closer.

To understand how magnets do what they do we need to be able to 'see' these force fields.

We can see the shape of the force fields with the help of small particles of crushed iron called **iron filings**.

Experiment

Try this simple experiment using bar magnets and iron filings.

1 Place a bar magnet under a sheet of A4 paper.

2 Sprinkle iron filings lightly on to the paper and gently tap the paper until the iron filings arrange themselves along the 'lines of magnetic force'.

3 Repeat the procedure with *two* bar magnets under the paper, first with a north pole and a south pole close to each other and then with two north poles (or south poles) close to each other.

4 Discuss what you observe with your teacher.

5 When you have finished, ask your teacher to give you a selection of different metals (e.g. iron, nickel, copper, aluminium). Find out which metals are attracted to a magnet and which are not.

Field patterns

The magnetic field around a typical bar magnet is shown in the following diagram.

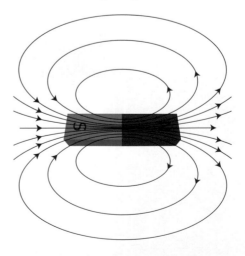

Magnetic fields

Lines of force 'start' at the north pole and 'end' at the south pole. The arrows indicate the direction of the lines of magnetic force and always point **from north to south**.

When two north poles or two south poles are brought close together they **repel**. The magnetic field in this case has the following appearance.

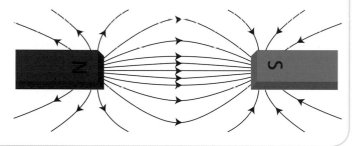

When a north pole and a south pole are brought close together they attract. The magnetic field in this case has the following appearance.

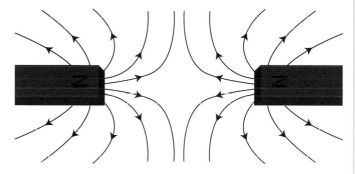

Supermagnets!

Magnets can vary in strength and the strength of a magnet can be judged from a diagram like this.

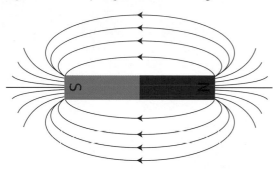

A weak magnet has a weak field and is represented by few field lines which are spaced well apart. A stong magnet has a strong field and is represented by many field lines which are closely spaced.

Some magnets can be made which are very strong.

They are often called **supermagnets** and are made from a soft shiny metal called **neodymium**.

neodymium magnets

Neodymium magnets are amongst the strongest permanent magnets known. Small neodymium supermagnets are used widely in microphones, loudspeakers, in-ear headphones and computer hard drives.

⟹

Supermagnets!

Larger supermagnets are used in the powerful electric motors of hybrid cars.

the electric motor in a hybrid car

How does this work?

Your teacher may be able to demonstrate an interesting experiment with a small neodymium magnet and a length of copper pipe.

Drop a small steel nut from the top of the tube and catch it when it emerges at the bottom.

Now do the same thing with a small neodymium magnet of about the same size. The result is quite surprising! The magnet falls through the tube, but at a very slow speed.

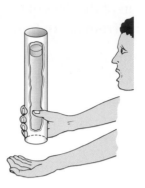

The explanation is quite complicated. Ask your physics teacher if you want to find out how it works.

You can consult this website for other interesting supermagnet experiments:

http://amasci.com/neodemo.html

Electromagnets

A problem with permanent magnets is that they cannot be switched on and off. However, there is another type of magnet which *can* be switched on and off.

An **electromagnet** can be constructed quite simply.

A length of wire is coiled around a piece of iron and then an electric current is passed through this coil. The electric current which flows through the coil of wire creates a magnetic field which is very similar to the field around a bar magnet. (You can check this by placing a sheet of paper over the coil and sprinkling iron filings, as before.)

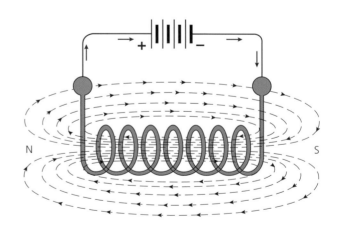

You can build an electromagnet of your own. All you need is a battery, a length of insulated wire and an iron nail.

Its construction is shown in the following diagram.

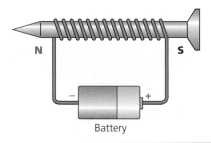

build your own electromagnet

An electromagnet has another great advantage over a permanent magnet – its strength can be controlled.

You can investigate the physical factors which determine the strength of an electromagnet by carrying out the following practical investigation.

Experiment

There are three factors which we can investigate.

1 The number of turns of wire

1 Construct an electromagnet with the wire coiled round the nail, say, 5 times. (The nail is called the **core** of the electromagnet.)

2 Connect it to a battery and then lower the head of the nail into a heap of paperclips.

3 Raise the electromagnet and count the number of paperclips which it has managed to lift. Repeat this a few times to achieve an **average** number.

4 Now repeat the same procedure after winding the wire around the nail 10 times.

5 Continue increasing the number of turns and counting the number of paperclips which can be lifted.

2 The strength of the electric current

1 Construct an electromagnet with a suitable number of turns of wire.

2 Connect this to a single 1.5 V battery and pick up and count paperclips as before.

3 Now connect to two 1.5 V batteries (3 V) and repeat.

(Increasing the number of batteries increases the voltage supplied, which in turn increases the electric current flowing in the coil of wire.)

4 Repeat with three batteries (4.5 V) and four batteries (6 V). **Do not go beyond 6 V!**

You can improve this experiment by including an **ammeter** in the circuit. This allows you to **measure** the electric current supplied by one, two, three and four batteries. You might then draw a graph of the average number or paperclips lifted (*y*-axis) against the size of the current (*x*-axis).

(Good housekeeping – do not leave your electromagnet switched on for a long period. You will 'flatten' the batteries and ruin your experiment.)

3 The metal core – no help this time?

Can you perform an experiment to investigate what happens to the strength of an electromagnet if you change the metal which is used for the core?

(You can even investigate non-metal cores such as plastic.)
Discuss with your teacher.

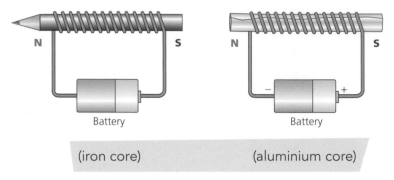

(iron core) (aluminium core)

Conclusion

A strong electromagnet can be produced therefore by

- having a large number of turns of wire in the coil

- using a large electric current

- winding the coil on a metal core (usually iron).

Powerful electromagnets attached to cranes are used in scrap
yards and steelworks. In these places heavy steel objects have
to be moved frequently. Steel objects like scrap cars can be
picked up, transferred, and dropped at another location.

Magnetic resonance imaging (MRI) scans

Take a look on the inside!

Doctors often need to be able to see inside our bodies when they
suspect there is something going on which isn't quite as it should
be. This might be with our bones or internal organs.

You may think the best way of doing this is to take an X-ray
photograph.

The problem is that a **single** X-ray can only show our skeletons
(hard tissue).

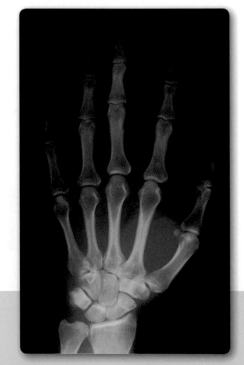

Internal organs and muscles (soft tissue) can be revealed by a **CT scan**. However this involves a concentrated dose of X-rays delivered from several angles.

A full-body CT scan is equivalent to about 100 conventional X-rays! Unfortunately, over-exposure to X-rays can damage healthy tissue in our bodies, so it is important to limit the number of X-rays to which we are exposed. This then becomes a problem if doctors need to collect lots of detailed information either through taking a large number of X-rays, or several CT scans.

Magnetic resonance imaging (MRI) scans can now overcome these problems.

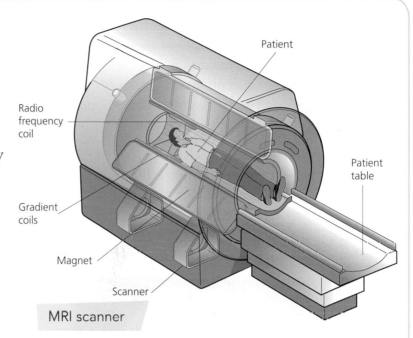

Radio frequency coil

Gradient coils

Magnet

Scanner

Patient

Patient table

MRI scanner

How do MRI scans work?

The MRI machine produces exceptionally strong magnetic forces, or force fields.

Our bodies are made up mainly of water so if a patient is placed inside a strong magnetic field, the water molecules in the body 'line up' along the force field lines, just like the iron filings lined up in the earlier experiment.

A radio signal is then sent through the 'tunnel' where the patient is located (see the last photograph).

The forces generated by the combination of radio waves and the strong magnetic field cause the water molecules to spin!

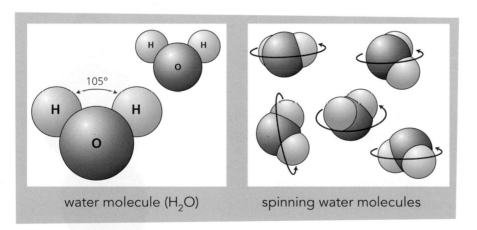

105°

water molecule (H_2O)

spinning water molecules

Magnetic resonance imaging (MRI) scans

The amazing thing is that water molecules spin at different rates in different types of tissue. A computer can be programmed to detect these different spin rates and so produce pictures of different tissues. MRI scans can therefore produce a detailed picture of soft tissue inside the body.

The great advantage of using MRI scans is that doctors don't have to worry about the harmful effects to healthy tissue which can occur with over-exposure to X-rays. When the MRI scan is completed the water molecules in the body simply settle back into their normal positions.

The MRI room

The magnetic field generated by the scanner is so strong that it is housed in a large secure room.

No one is allowed to wear metal objects such as watches, jewellery, or even to have keys in pockets, as they might be ripped from the body by the enormous attractive force. Patients who have been fitted with electronic pacemakers or artificial (metal) joints, such as hip joints, are not permitted to have MRI scans.

Firemen receive special training on how to deal with a fire in an MRI room. They must not enter the room carrying a fireman's axe. The consequences could be lethal!

The Institute of Physics has produced very informative interactive animations which show four different ways in which modern technology can help doctors 'see' inside the human body. View these at this link:

www.insidestory.iop.org/insidestory_flash1.html

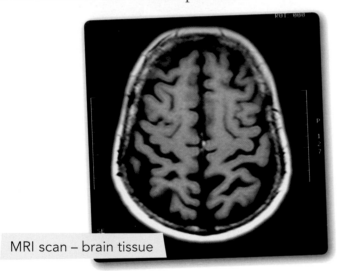

MRI scan – brain tissue

Where am I?

MRI scanning is a very modern and high-tech application of magnetism. There are, however, more traditional ways of making good use of magnets.

Throughout the centuries people have used magnets to help them navigate. We are all familiar with **navigation compasses** although most of us don't really know how to use one!

A magnetic compass needle aligns itself along the magnetic field lines of the Earth and always points to **magnetic north** on Earth.

This gives hillwalkers and sailors a fixed reference from which all other directions can be measured.

Even though seafaring navigators now have satellite positioning systems, which can pinpoint the position of a ship at sea to within a few metres, they still have a ship's compass on board in case the satellite signal should fail.

You can learn a lot more about the history of navigation at sea and the use of compasses, using the following link:

www.nmm.ac.uk/explore/sea-and-ships/facts/ships-and-seafarers/the-magnetic-compass

Magnetic variation

You will have noticed in the photograph of the Earth's magnetic field that **magnetic north** and **geographic north** (also known as **true north**) are not in the same position. Anyone who uses a compass to navigate must be aware of this.

The Earth actually behaves like a giant bar magnet with a north pole and a south pole, but this imaginary giant magnet inside the Earth does not point 'straight up' towards geographic north. It is tilted a few degrees to one side as shown overleaf. This means that all our compass needles are pointing to magnetic north and so hillwalkers have to allow for this when measuring the **bearings** they wish to follow on a hike.

The angle between magnetic north and true (geographic) north is called the **angle of declination** and it has different values at different locations on the Earth's surface.

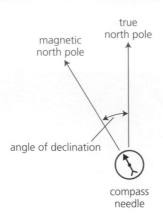

Another complication is that the angle of declination is continually changing by a small amount. This is typically one twelfth of a degree every year, 'swinging' slowly from **west** of true north to **east** of true north and back again!

Maps

Ordnance Survey maps usually quote the angle of declination in any area at the time of printing. For this reason, it is not a good idea to plan a hike in the hills using a 20 year-old map. You could miss your intended destination by a country mile or two!

Our modern day technology uses geo-positioning satellites (GPS) and accurate OS maps to provide us with reliable maps which can be loaded onto our mobile phones. (No more wrestling with a large map swirling around in the wind, although a paper map doesn't need a fully charged battery!)

Maps are quite fascinating and you can find out about the history of Ordnance Survey maps and some other amazing facts about maps by following this link:

www.ordnancesurvey.co.uk/oswebsite/media/features/introos/

Setting a bearing with a map and compass is not really too difficult. If you would like to learn how to do this then try this link:

www.abc-of-hiking.com/navigation-skills/compass-navigation.asp

The magnetosphere – our protector

The Earth's magnetic field, known as the **magnetosphere**, extends between 60 and 70 thousand kilometres into Space in the direction of the Sun, and twice that distance in the opposite direction.

Thus the magnetosphere is not spherical as the name suggests. Its curious shape is actually due to the combination of the Earth's internal magnetic field and the **solar wind**.

The solar wind is a stream of charged particles (mainly protons and electrons) which flow outwards from the Sun. This stream of charged particles is called **plasma.** You can observe plasma by simply playing around with a plasma ball, a toy which is quite common in gadget shops.

The Sun's plasma hurtles towards the Earth at a speed of 400 km s^{-1} and could kill many living things on Earth.

The charged particles in the plasma are deflected by the Earth's magnetosphere however and are prevented from penetrating to the surface of the planet. Without this protection, life as we know it could not survive on Earth.

a dangerous star

our protector

Astronomers and physicists believe there is enough evidence to suggest that Mars once had oceans and an atmosphere. They believe however that Mars lost both due to the direct impact of the solar wind because it did not have a strong and stable magnetosphere to protect it.

The magnetosphere – our protector

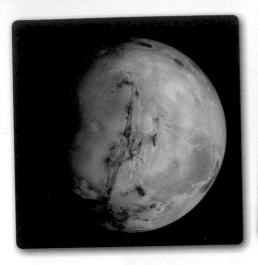 

While we find magnets interesting and we can put magnetism to good use it is quite daunting to realise that without magnetism our Planet Earth could be a lifeless place!

QUESTIONS

1 Identify and research five objects in everyday use that involve magnets. (You might want to research headphones, electric motors, speakers, compasses, screwdrivers, buttons on handbags, or cupboard or wardrobe doors.) Produce a report of your findings.

2 Electromagnets can be switched on or off. List two devices that use electromagnets and explain why this is a useful feature.

3 Using the Internet or a reference book, find out what the cause of the Earth's magnetic field might be.

4 How does the Earth's magnetic field protect us?

GLOSSARY

Attract To cause objects to move towards each other

Magentic resonance imaging (MRI) A method of examining soft internal structures of the body

Magnetosphere The area surrounding the Earth influenced by the Earth's magnetic field

Repel To cause objects to move apart

FORCES, ELECTRICITY AND WAVES

Waves

11

The Electromagnetic Spectrum (a family of waves)

Level 3 — What came before?

 SCN 3-11b

By exploring radiations beyond the visible, I can describe a selected application, discussing the advantages and limitations.

Level 4 — What is this chapter about?

 SCN 4-11b

By carrying out a comparison of the properties of parts of the Electromagnetic Spectrum beyond the visible, I can explain the use of radiation and discuss how this has impacted upon society and our quality of life.

The Electromagnetic Spectrum

Chapter 1 in Book 3 introduced electromagnetic waves. Chapters 2 and 3 then discussed applications of waves from the different parts of the **Electromagnetic Spectrum**. This final Chapter of Book 4 returns to this very important area of physics and describes some additional applications of electromagnetic waves.

Visible light

James Clerk Maxwell, a brilliant Scottish mathematician and physicist, proposed that the **visible spectrum** (visible light), investigated by Sir Isaac Newton, was only a very small part of a much larger continuous spectrum of waves. Visible light is a spectrum within a spectrum.

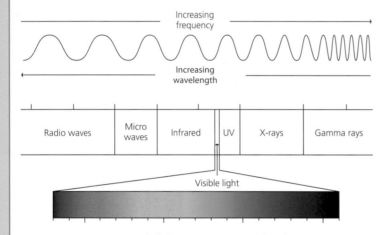

The Electromagnetic Spectrum!

This **Electromagnetic Spectrum** consists of lots of waves, most of which are invisible to us. These waves exist over a wide range of **wavelengths** and **frequencies**.

Despite the fact that the majority of waves in the Electromagnetic Spectrum cannot be *seen* by us, we can still *detect* them. In addition, scientists have found extremely clever ways of putting these waves to good use and so improve the quality of our lives.

We begin the chapter in the visible spectrum however and here we look at some applications of laser light.

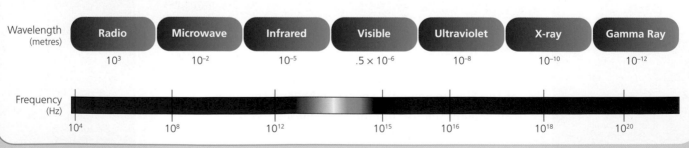

Laser light

Visible light is a small section of the Electromagnetic Spectrum and one very special form of visible light is laser light. When laser light was first discovered no-one knew what to do with it!

Today however, scientists and engineers have many applications for laser light.

Because all lasers have the property of producing light which is very intense, highly directional and focused, they find many applications. Here are some of the ways in which we make use of them.

Laser eye surgery

The use of lasers in medicine has changed the lives of many people for the better.

Some people suffer from **diabetes** which is an imbalance of sugar level in the blood. Diabetes can lead to bleeding of tiny blood vessels in the eye which supply the retina with oxygen. This is called **diabetic retinopathy** and in extreme cases it can result in blindness.

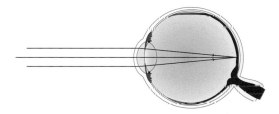

Laser beam

Laser spots

Macula

Diabetic retinopathy

A laser beam can be directed through the pupil of the eye and aimed at the damaged blood vessels in the retina. Pulses of laser energy then burn the

blood vessels and so seal them. Some loss of retinal surface occurs due to the burn spots, but the bleeding is stopped and the patient's vision can be saved.

Today, the term 'laser eye surgery' is more commonly associated with the procedure which is designed to improve the eye's ability to focus light.

The cornea and lens in the eye work together to refract and focus light on the retina.

People who need to wear spectacles because they are long-sighted or short-sighted might prefer to pay for laser surgery. This involves using a fine laser beam to burn away thin concentric layers of the cornea, altering its curvature so that light is focused correctly. After successful laser surgery there is no need to wear spectacles.

Port wine stains

Sometimes known as 'birthmarks', port wine stains can be removed very successfully by laser treatment.

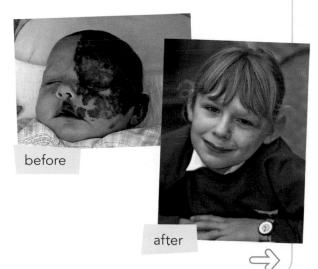

before

after

About three in every 1000 babies are born with port wine stains, most of which occur on the face. These stains (or birthmarks) are caused by tiny blood vessels, called capillaries, which are abnormally dilated. This means that they are wider than they should be and too much blood is supplied to the surface of the skin. The result is a red or purple area of skin tissue.

A beam of laser light can be directed at the affected area to destroy the abnormal capillaries, so cutting off the excessive blood supply. Several sessions of laser treatment are required as only small areas of skin are treated at each session.

The procedure is most effective when applied to young children. Babies as young as two months may be treated.

Similar laser treatment can be used to eradicate unwanted tattoos from the skin. This can be expensive, so think carefully before deciding to have a tattoo!

Other applications

Laser light beams are used too in CD players, optical fibres and spirit levels. They are also used to cut metal plate accurately, read bar-codes at your local supermarket and entertain us with 'laser shows'. The list of applications is large.

5 051146 000282

Infrared waves

Infrared (IR) waves have wavelengths slightly longer than the wavelength of visible red light (700 nm). Our eyes cannot see infrared radiation but our skin can detect the wave energy. This is because infrared wave energy is converted to heat energy when **absorbed** by a surface. In fact, infrared waves are sometimes nicknamed 'heat waves'.

Warm or hot objects also **radiate** infrared waves. The Earth heats up when it absorbs IR radiation which has travelled across Space from the Sun, and cools down by re-radiating IR waves back into Space.

Weather watching

People are often prone to criticise weather forecasts, but the reality is that the scientists who observe and study weather are fairly accurate when predicting short-term weather trends. This is mainly due to the stream of data received from weather satellites, most of which are in geostationary and polar orbits.

Infrared waves

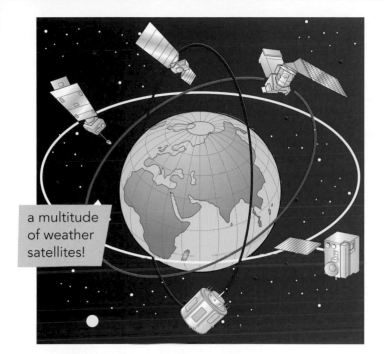

a multitude of weather satellites!

photograph of a hurricane

IR photograph of the Earth

These satellites take photographs of weather patterns continuously. However when parts of the Earth are in darkness, normal photographs are impossible and the satellites switch automatically to infrared cameras.

Infrared cameras detect differences in the **temperatures** of land, sea and clouds to produce infrared photographs which assist with weather observation.

Even more spectacular photographs are produced when we take infrared photographs of stars and galaxies!

infrared photograph of the 'local' Universe

This photograph was taken through a satellite telescope and shows the infrared radiation being emitted by galaxies in a large section of our Universe. The white band in the centre shows more of our own galaxy, The Milky Way, which contains *half a billion stars*. The remainder of the photograph has captured infrared radiation from *one and a half billion galaxies* beyond The Milky Way!

When viewed like this Space isn't quite as empty as perhaps you thought it was!

Ease my pain!

Closer to home, we can put infrared wave energy to good use. An infrared lamp can be a very useful piece of equipment when we have muscular injuries or strains. Sportsmen and sportswomen use IR lamps regularly when they suffer sports injuries.

Remember that IR radiation is converted to heat energy when absorbed. Muscle injuries are known to heal more quickly when exposed to infrared radiation.

Can we make use of the fact that our bodies also **radiate** infrared waves?

The answer, not surprisingly, is yes!

Medical thermography

In Book 3, Chapter 4, we stated that infrared imaging can be used to detect cancerous tumours in the human body. Our bodies continually generate heat energy and different parts of the body are at different temperatures. Particular physical problems can produce higher temperatures where they occur. **Thermal imaging** can pinpoint the area affected and so assist doctors with diagnosis.

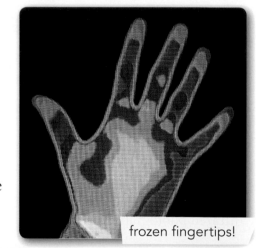

frozen fingertips!

The equipment consists basically of an infrared camera and a computer. Usually, the computer is programmed to colour-code the range of temperatures from 10°C to 55°C. The system is capable of converting the radiation detected into temperature measurements with an accuracy of 0.1°C!

IR monitoring of blood flow

Cooler areas are generally shown in blue with warmer areas in yellow and red.

If a medical problem has developed inside the body, medical **thermography**, known as **digital infrared thermal imaging (DITI)**, will usually locate the source.

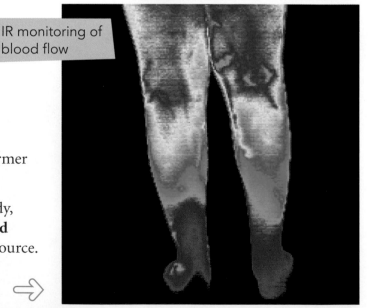

For example, DITI can easily detect the flow of warm blood through the body.

The monitoring of blood flow makes thermal imaging an ideal tool for detecting a **deep vein thrombosis (DVT)**, a serious blood clot which can develop in the leg.

DITI is used to detect and observe a wide range of other medical conditions, including arthritis, spinal defects, cancerous tumours, skin defects and even dental problems.

What's on the other channel?

The remote control which we use to change channels on the television is just an infrared transmitter. It sends an invisible beam of IR radiation to a receiver in the TV.

IR signals of slightly different frequencies and wavelengths provide us with a range of remote control functions such as channel change, volume, brightness and contrast.

Try this!

(i) Your own infrared camera

You are probably familiar with taking photographs or videos with your mobile phone. You probably don't know however that your mobile's photographic system is sensitive to infrared radiation, just like the IR camera in a weather satellite! You can prove this by setting your mobile phone to *video mode*. Ask a friend to point the TV remote control toward you and press a button. If you look at the remote through the screen on your mobile phone you will see a flash of light! (Without the use of your mobile you won't see anything, because infrared radiation is invisible to us.)

(ii) Infrared thermometer – practical challenge

Your physics department is likely to have infrared thermometers like the one shown.

infrared thermometer

radiation cans

Infrared waves

You can investigate which type of surface (dull black, dull white, or silvery white) is best at radiating infrared waves as follows:

1 Fill the metal or plastic radiation cans with hot water and point the IR thermometer at each can in turn.

2 Take temperature measurements of each can at regular time intervals. (If you don't have access to infrared thermometers you can use conventional liquid-in-glass thermometers instead – as shown in the second photograph.)

3 Plot temperature–time graphs (cooling curves) of your results.

4 Discuss with your partners what the cooling curves mean, in terms of infrared radiation.

Modern applications of radio waves – radar

Beyond infrared radiation in the Electromagnetic Spectrum (and in order of increasing wavelength) we find the microwave band. Beyond microwaves we have **radar**, then TV and finally radio waves. There are no hard and fast divisions between these bands but they provide a useful way of dividing up the continuous spectrum.

In this section we look at radar waves.

These can be thought of either as very short wavelength radio waves or as long wavelength microwaves.

As a rough guide we are referring to wavelengths in the region of 1 m and frequency of the order of 10^8 Hz.

Many people believe that radar (RAdio Detection And Ranging) was developed by Britain during the Second World War, but scientists and engineers had observed in the early 1900s that radio waves could be affected by distant metallic objects. The radio waves affected could then be used to determine the positions of the objects. No one had investigated the possibilities seriously until the 1930s, but with war looming the possibility of being able to detect distant enemy aeroplanes meant resources were allocated to research and development. Much of this work was secretive and this limited general knowledge about its development.

The person most credited with the development of British radar was Sir Robert Alexander Watson Watt (1892–1973). He was born in Brechin and educated at St Andrews University. He was a descendant of James Watt and responsible for the setting up of the **Chain Home System**. This was a series of radio towers along the east coast of Britain which could detect the incoming enemy aircraft.

You can read more about this at the following website.

www.anti-aircraft.co.uk/chain_home_map.html

Originally the detection system was referred to as the Range and Direction Finding System (RDF).

This gave no indication of using radio waves as its means of operation. It was later that the term radar became accepted almost universally.

Germany already had a much more sophisticated radar system at that time but the British one was integrated into an effective command and control system which allowed fighters to scramble and meet the enemy within a very short time.

Our modern lives are much affected by radar and some of the more obvious examples are discussed in this chapter.

Principles of radar

A radar system has a transmitter that emits radio waves in certain directions.

When these waves make contact with an object they are reflected and scattered in many directions. The waves are reflected better by materials which are better at electrical conducting. This includes metals, seawater and wet clouds.

Some of the waves are reflected back to the detector and the signal received can be used to give an indication of an object's direction, position and speed.

The size, strength and quality of the reflected signal depends on a number of things, but in general a square cornered box shape is very good for reflecting radar waves back to the detector. Many ships and yachts have these corner reflectors fitted to their masts to make sure that they can be identified easily by radar in poor visibility conditions.

Uses of radar

Air Traffic Control

Air Traffic Control uses radar to monitor the movement of aeroplanes and helicopters in our airspace. Most airports have a central control RADAR which rotates and 'sweeps' the area around it. It can detect aircraft and monitor their movements until landing, or leaving our airspace. It has the simple *primary* radar which reflects off all large objects and also *secondary* radar which detects a signal automatically transmitted for the aircraft via a device on board called a **transponder**. The transponder detects the primary radar and then emits a special signal which gives its own basic information. This transponder is also used by military aircraft so that if they fly over 'friendly' radar, their transponders tell the people on the ground not to fire at them. This military system is called IFF (Identification Friend or Foe).

Navigational radars

These radars transmit 'short' wavelengths in the 3 cm to 10 cm range. Such short wavelengths reflect from stone and/or earth as well as metallic objects. These are common on ships and long range commercial aircraft as they can show coastal outlines and can also determine heavy rain or rough sea conditions. It is not uncommon on a long flight for the aircraft captain to put the seat belt warning lights on if he/she detects some rough conditions ahead using this radar.

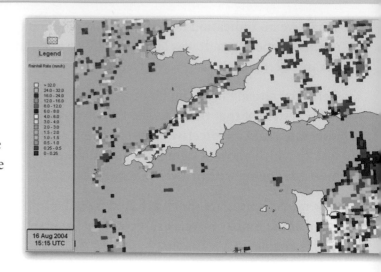

Weather sensing radar

Weather sensing radar uses radio waves to determine precipitation in an area. Once found it can determine the type (rain, snow, hail), calculate its intensity and forecast its movement over an area. This is particularly important if there are likely to be very heavy falls of rain or snow. It may lead to flood forecasting or evacuation warnings depending upon the severity.

The weather map is generally overlaid on an existing map of an area and the severity of the rainfall will be denoted by a colour. This allows us to see the progress of a storm as it passes through an area.

Military radar

There are two types of radar employed in military operations. These are detection radar and targeting radar.

Detection radars

Detection radars scan wide areas. For example the Chain Home network scanned the eastern coast of Britain during the Second World War. These detection radars are large scale devices which cover hundreds of miles seeking out evidence of any military activity. Some 'early warning' radar systems are ground-based and can be seen around the country. They look like very large golf balls and can detect very distant objects such as missiles or aircraft heading towards us.

These are static structures and can only look for things which are heading in our general direction.

We also have airborne early warning radar using aircraft. For many years Britain developed its own version built into *Nimrod* aircraft but it was beset by technical difficulties and we now use the American *Boeing* E-3 Sentry system.

The photograph shows the AEW aircraft with the radar disc visible.

Modern applications of radio waves – radar

The aircraft have the advantage over the static radar in that they can hover over an area anywhere in the world and transmit real-time information to people on the ground.

Targeting radars

These radars use the same principle as detection radars but can scan a much narrower area. They are used to detect enemy ships, aircraft or missiles. The information from the radar is then used by other systems to attack with bombs or missiles.

Radar guns

These are handheld or static devices used to measure the speed of moving traffic.

They send out a radio signal which is reflected from a vehicle and this reflection can tell us quite accurately how fast that vehicle is moving. It uses a very narrow beam and so needs to be pointed directly at the object in question to determine its speed.

Radar guns are also used to measure speeds at sports events such as tennis serves and cricket bowling.

There are many devices which car drivers can buy now to detect when a radar beam is present. This means a speeding driver can slow down and avoid breaking the speed limit. These devices are not quite legal and there is uncertainty as to whether they should be allowed in cars.

Ultraviolet radiation

Having looked at the radiations beyond the red end of the visible spectrum (infrared and radar) we now look at the radiation just on the far side of the violet end of the spectrum.

Ultraviolet radiations have lower wavelengths and higher frequencies than any visible light. Like infrared, ultraviolet radiations are invisible to the human eye.

As you may recall from Book 3 Chapter 2, ultraviolet radiation (UV) is a known major cause of skin cancer. However UV also has applications which can improve our health and also our quality of life. We now look at some of these.

Treat those spots!

The harmful effects of UV radiation can be used successfully to kill bacteria which cause skin blemishes such as acne and psoriasis. UV-A type radiation is normally used for this kind of treatment. (You may recall from Book 3 that ultraviolet radiation can be classified as UVA, UVB, or UVC. Type A has the highest frequency and shortest wavelength. The Sun's radiation has all three types but all of the UVC and much of the UVB is absorbed in our atmosphere.)

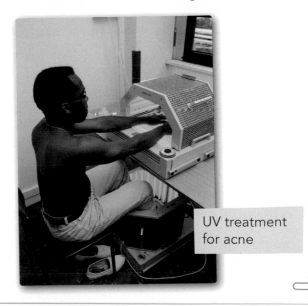

UV treatment for acne

Sterilisation

Because certain wavelengths of ultraviolet are so effective at killing bacteria, the radiation can be used to sterilise surgical instruments in a 'UV oven'.

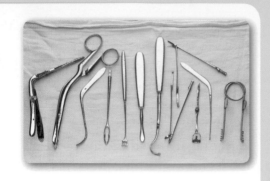

A little UV is actually good for us

1 A common application of ultraviolet is in the treatment of new-born babies for **jaundice**. This is a liver condition which affects the blood and causes the skin and eyes to develop a yellow appearance. However a short time in a UV incubator is usually an effective way of correcting the chemical imbalance in the blood.

2 Limited exposure to ultraviolet radiation also helps our bodies to make **vitamin D**. This is most important because vitamin D helps our bodies to absorb calcium and ensures strong and healthy bones. Ironically, vitamin D also builds up our resistance to … development of cancer!

UV beads – practical challenge

UV beads change colour when exposed to ultraviolet radiation. You can observe this effect by simply placing a few beads on a window ledge when there is a reasonable amount of sunshine. They are amazing!

Now ask your science teacher to help you set up this experiment to test and compare various sun-creams. The procedure is as follows.

1 Smear a biological glass plate with a film of sun-cream.

2 Place the plate above a number of UV beads.

3 Place a UV lamp above the plate and shine UV through the plate, towards the beads.

4 Note how many beads change colour.

5 Repeat the experiment for different grades (skin protection factor) of sun-creams.

When you are planning this investigation you must discuss the factors in the procedure which will ensure a 'fair test'.

You can now use the web to discover what the term 'skin protection factor' means.

UV beads

X-rays

You will recall from Book 3 that **X-ray** was the name given to the then unknown radiation discovered by Wilhelm Röntgen in 1895. This radiation is a very high frequency radiation whose wavelength is shorter than that of any ultraviolet radiation.

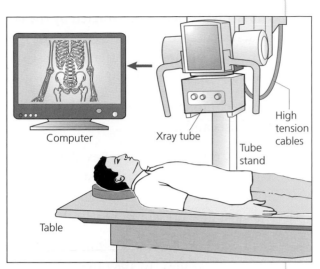

The scientific name for an X-ray photograph is a **radiograph** and these provided the first method of 'seeing' inside the body without the need to operate.

A conventional X-ray photograph is taken by positioning the patient in front of a photographic film. A short burst of X-radiation is then aimed at the patient. The photographic film is darkened, or fogged, when X-rays strike it. Areas which do not receive X-rays are not fogged.

Since bone tissue does not allow the X-rays to reach the film our skeleton appears white when the film is developed. Any crack in a bone will appear black since the X-radiation will pass through it and so fog the film.

Computerised tomography (CT)

CT scanning uses an all-round array of X-ray machines built into a kind of tunnel into which the patient is pushed slowly.

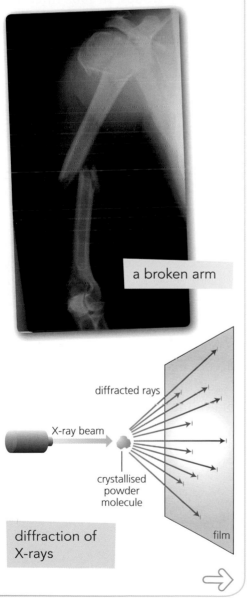

a broken arm

A CT scan is capable of generating 3-D pictures of our skeletons and also pictures of **soft tissue**. This is why CT scanners are commonly used to examine brain tissue.

X-ray crystallography

Scientists are able to investigate the structure of crystal lattices in solids by crushing them into powder form and then passing X-rays through the powder. The X-rays are deflected around the atoms in the crystal structure. This is called **diffraction**.

(Diffraction of radio waves was explained in Book 3, Chapter 3).

diffraction of X-rays

X-rays

The X-rays which are diffracted by the layers of atoms in the crystal structure produce a pattern of spots on a photographic film. By analysing the pattern of these spots, scientists can then work out the arrangement of atoms within the crystal.

This technique has been used extensively by chemists, biologists, physicists and geologists.

In 1953, probably the most exciting structure ever was revealed by X-ray diffraction. It was the structure of **DNA**, the building block of life! The term DNA is an abbreviation of deoxyribonucleic acid – a substance present in nearly all living organisms.

DNA was found to have a **double-helix** structure of sugar and phosphate groups. In 1962 three scientists, Frances Crick, James Watson and Maurice Wilkins, were recognised for their work in unlocking the mysterious structure of DNA and shared the Nobel Prize for Physiology/Medicine.

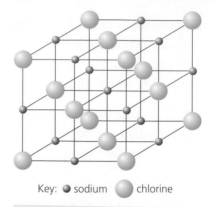

Key: ● sodium ⬤ chlorine

crystal structure of common salt (sodium chloride)

structure of DNA

Crick, Watson and Wilkins

Since 1962 much experimental research has given scientists a deeper understanding of how DNA works and has led to exciting breakthroughs in all areas of biological sciences such as forensics, biotechnology, genetic engineering and gene therapy.

Gamma radiation

As you may recall from Book 3, Chapter 2 gamma radiation is *very* high frequency radiation with the shortest wavelengths of all electromagnetic waves. (Frequencies exceed 10^{19} Hz and wavelengths are less than 10^{-12} m.) These high energy waves originate from stars and galaxies and so are sometimes called **cosmic waves**. However they are also emitted by the nuclei of certain radioactive atoms here on Earth.

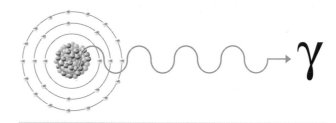

gamma emission from the nucleus of an atom

Gamma rays are even more penetrating than X-rays and can only be absorbed effectively by dense metals like lead. However the lead has to be several centimetres thick.

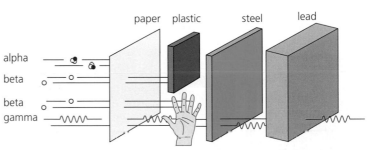

Gamma radiation, like many electromagnetic waves, is harmful to living tissue and can cause cancer. Strangely however it is also useful for the **treatment** of cancerous tumours in the human body because the radiation damages the DNA in the cancerous cells and kills them.

Radiotherapy

(i) External radiotherapy

This is the medical term used to describe the treatment of cancer by gamma radiation. One technique involves aiming a beam of gamma rays at a tumour. The location of the tumour has to be pin-pointed very accurately beforehand.

The machine directs a beam of radiation towards the cancerous area. It is designed to rotate **around** the body so that surrounding healthy tissue receives a minimum dose of radiation whilst the tumour receives a maximum dose.

Cobalt-60 is a radioactive isotope commonly used in the treatment of brain tumours.

(ii) Internal radiotherapy

Another technique involves introducing a **radio-isotope** directly into the affected area.

Cancer of the thyroid gland can be treated by this procedure.

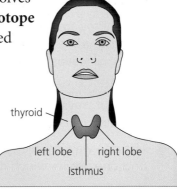

The radioactive isotope **iodine-131** can be taken as a drink or capsule, or injected into the bloodstream. The thyroid gland (in the throat) absorbs this radioactive isotope which then begins the process of killing cancerous cells.

During this treatment the patient becomes temporarily radioactive and has to be isolated for about 3 days in a separate room!

Radioactive tracers

In some diagnostic procedures low-level radioactive isotopes can be introduced into the bloodstream and followed as they travel around the body. The movement of the 'tracer' can be monitored by a **gamma camera** placed above the body.

The radio-isotope **technetium-99** can be injected directly into the kidneys.

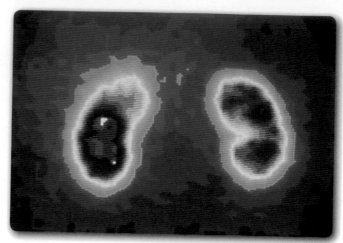

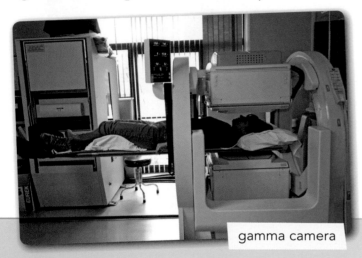

gamma camera

Gamma radiation passes out through the body and is detected by a gamma camera. Detection of, say, a problem blockage in the kidneys is then possible due to a concentrated build-up of the radioactive tracer.

QUESTIONS

1　📖 Prepare a poster on the Electromagnetic Spectrum showing the range of waves and their properties or uses.

2　List four ways in which electromagnetic radiation is used for medical purposes.

3　List one way in which UV is helpful to you and one way in which it is harmful to you.

4　Describe, in detail, one use of radio waves.

5　📖 Prepare a small report on James Clerk Maxwell. You should include where he came from, what he was famous for and any other interesting points you discover about him.

GLOSSARY

Double-helix The shape of the atomic structure of DNA (deoxyribonucleic acid); hugely significant in science

Electromagnetic Spectrum The range of electromagnetic radiation from radio waves to gamma rays

Jaundice A medical condition of the liver which can affect skin colour

Radar Radio detection and ranging

Radiograph The medical term for an X-ray photograph

Radiotherapy The treatment of medical conditions by radiation

Thermography The imaging of an area of the body which shows the temperature across the area

Index

Index

Curriculum for Excellence mapping grid

Curriculum for Excellence Science Level 4 Experiences and Outcomes

Strand	Outcome	1	2	3	4	5	6	7	8	9	10	11
Planet Earth	SCN 4-01a											
Planet Earth	SCN 4-02a											
Planet Earth	SCN 4-02b											
Planet Earth	SCN 4-03a											
Planet Earth	SCN 4-04a	■										
Planet Earth	SCN 4-04b	■										
Planet Earth	SCN 4-05a		■									
Planet Earth	SCN 4-05b											
Planet Earth	SCN 4-06a				■							
Forces, Electricity and Waves	SCN 4-07a									■		
Forces, Electricity and Waves	SCN 4-07b									■		
Forces, Electricity and Waves	SCN 4-08a										■	
Forces, Electricity and Waves	SCN 4-08b			■								
Forces, Electricity and Waves	SCN 4-09a					■						
Forces, Electricity and Waves	SCN 4-09b						■					
Forces, Electricity and Waves	SCN 4-09c						■					
Forces, Electricity and Waves	SCN 4-10a											
Forces, Electricity and Waves	SCN 4-10b											
Forces, Electricity and Waves	SCN 4-11a							■	■			
Forces, Electricity and Waves	SCN 4-11b											■
Biological Systems	SCN 4-12a											
Biological Systems	SCN 4-12b											
Biological Systems	SCN 4-13a											
Biological Systems	SCN 4-13b											
Biological Systems	SCN 4-13c											
Biological Systems	SCN 4-14a											
Biological Systems	SCN 4-14b											
Biological Systems	SCN 4-14c											
Materials	SCN 4-15a											
Materials	SCN 4-16a											
Materials	SCN 4-16b											
Materials	SCN 4-17a											
Materials	SCN 4-18a											
Materials	SCN 4-19a											
Materials	SCN 4-19b											
Topical Science	SCN 4-20a											
Topical Science	SCN 4-20b											